# SOUTHERN
# CALIFORNIA

**MICHAEL'S GUIDE SERIES INCLUDES:**

MICHAEL'S GUIDE ARGENTINA, CHILE, PARAGUAY
&URUGUAY
MICHAEL'S GUIDE BOLIVIA & PERU
MICHAEL'S GUIDE ECUADOR, COLOMBIA & VENEZUELA
MICHAEL'S GUIDE BRAZIL
MICHAEL'S GUIDE SOUTH AMERICA (Continental)

MICHAEL'S GUIDE NORTHERN CALIFORNIA
MICHAEL'S GUIDE SOUTHERN CALIFORNIA
MICHAEL'S GUIDE CALIFORNIA

MICHAEL'S GUIDE SCANDINAVIA
MICHAEL'S GUIDE SCOTLAND
MICHAEL'S GUIDE SWITZERLAND
MICHAEL'S GUIDE HUNGARY
MICHAEL'S GUIDE TURKEY

MICHAEL'S GUIDE NEW YORK CITY
MICHAEL'S GUIDE LONDON
MICHAEL'S GUIDE PARIS
MICHAEL'S GUIDE AMSTERDAM
MICHAEL'S GUIDE BRUSSELS & ANTWERP
MICHAEL'S GUIDE FRANKFURT
MICHAEL'S GUIDE ROME
MICHAEL'S GUIDE MADRID
MICHAEL'S GUIDE BARCELONA
MICHAEL'S GUIDE JERUSALEM

# SOUTHERN CALIFORNIA

Series editor:
Michael Shichor

*I* NBAL
Travel Information Ltd.

Inbal Travel Information Ltd.
P.O.Box 39090 Tel Aviv Israel 61390

©1990 edition

**Intl. ISBN 965-288-059-0**

Photos: The Californias
         Michelle Menna

**Distributed in the United Kingdom by:**
Kuperard (London) Ltd.
30 Cliff Rd.
London NW1 9AG

**U.K. ISBN 1-870668-33-2**

# $C$ONTENTS

# $T$ABLE OF MAPS

## Preface

California, the 'Golden State' of America, is a legendary land of promise where anything is possible. It has attracted gold-hunters. nature lovers, loners and revolutionaries, radical reformers, refugees, waves of immigarants. and a perennial stream of tourists wanting to taste the good life.

California's extraordinary beauty and pleasant climate are no doubt part of the attraction. California was the ultimate Western frontier, and today connections extend west beyond the Pacific to the Far East. It is a land rich in resources, and the most populaous state in the U.S.A, with a population of more than 23 million. Ninety-three percent of these people live in the metropolitan centers, but California also has some of the richest agricultural land in the U.S.A and the most productive economy. The clear. The clear skies, sunny climate and wide open spaces provide ideal conditions for the aerospace industry. and 'Silicon Valley' is a leading center for high technology. Hoolywood, the cradle of the film industry is still Mecca for thousands of actors, scripwriters, directors and comedians. The music industry also thrives here.

For the millions of tourists who visit California every year, the big attractions are the big inspiring natural wonders of the national parks, dramatic coastlines, golden beaches, haunting desert landscapes and misty cool forests, plus the excitement of metropolitan Los Angeles and San Francisco, and the magic of Disneyland.

We hope to introduce you to the many facets of California, and a variety of attractions in each area are presented, allowing the traveler to choose a choice, according to personal interest.

Our aim is to give you a deeper understanding of California, to help you plan a ideal trip, to lead you to the best and most exciting attractions, and to ensure that you derive maximum pleasure from your trip. We are sure that the effort invested in the compiling of this guide will be justiffied by your enhanced enjoyment.

## Using this Guide

In order to reap maximum benefit from the information concentrated in this Guide, we advise the traveler to carefully read the following advice. The facts contained in this book are meant to help the tourist find his or her way around, and to assure that he see the most, with maximum savings of money, time and effort.

The information contained in the Introduction should be read in its entirety as it has details which will help in making the earlh decisions and arrangements regarding hour trip. Reviewing the material thoroughly means that you will be better organized and set for your visit. Upon arrival in California you will already feel familiar and comfortable, more so than otherwise might have been the case.

The basic guideline in all MICHAEL'S GUIDE publications is to survey places in a primarily geographical sequence and not a thematic one. The logic behind it is that a geographical plan not only ensures the most efficient time use, but also contributes dramatically to getting to know an area and its different aspects as well as acquiring a feeling for it. Furthermore, you will be directed from a museum to a historical place, incorporating in your visit to one site several other locations which you may not have thought or heard of nor planned to visit.

The sections are accompanied by maps, especially designed to ease your way. Each chapter also includes a list of useful addresses and telephone numbers.

To further facilitate the use of this Guide, we have included an index, which includes all the major locations mentoned throughout the book. Consult the index to find something by name and it will refer you to the place where it is described in greatest detail.

Because times and places do change, an important rule when traveling in general, and when visitin California in particular, should be to consult the local sources of information. We have therefore accompanied nearly every place with a phone number for last minute checks and suggest you consult the hotel concierge, the local publications and newpapers, the tourist information offices, etc. All of them can advise you of the latest updated information at the specific time of your visit.

As for updating, a guide to a place like California cannot afford to march in place, and up to the time that the Guide went to press, we attempted to confim its relevance and up-to-dateness.

However, it is only natural that due to frequent changes which occur, travelers will find certain time-related facts somewhat less than precise when they arrive at their destination, and for this we apologize in advance.

To this end, cooperation and assistance is necessary and vital from those of you have enjoyed the information contained in this Guide. It ensures, first and foremost, that those who travel in your wake will also enjoy and succeed in their ventures as much as you have. For this purpose, we have included a short questionnaire at the end of this Guide and we will be most grateful to those who complete it and send it to us. A **complimentary copy** of the new edition will be forwardedto those of you who take the time, and whose contribution will apear in the updated edition.

During your visit you will see and experience many things — we have therefore left several blank pages at the back of this Guide. These are for you; to jot down those special experiences of people and places, feelings you may have had, or any other significant happenings along the way. You will always be able to look back on those words and remember.

Have a pleasant and exciting trip — Bon Voyage!

# *I*NTRODUCTION

## Part One — A First Taste of What's to Come

California is a multi-faceted gem. The gleam of each facet is only partial, yet together they create a strange, enticing and unique aura. This is a land of great physical beauty and contrasts, but the physical extremes are mild compared to the social, cultural and political ones. It is a land where the freedom of life-style can verge on the hedonistic, yet where religious sects with strict codes of behaviour flourish. It is a society generally tolerant of ethnic diversity, yet is marred by a history of vicious racial outbursts. It contains the agricultural heart of the nation, just an hour away from the nerve center of the microelectronics industry. It witnessed the birth of the modern conservation movement and shows a high degree of sensitivity to the environment, yet untempered greed and rampant exploitation have been driving forces in the growth of California. The land of bean sprouts and tofu, it also sustains the most gimmicky and greasy fast-food stands. Although the cauldron of the radicalism of the 1960s, California also gave the nation Richard Nixon and Ronald Reagan, two deeply conservative presidents. It is a land that has attracted dreamers, outcasts, desperate hopefuls, fugitives, artists, rebels, ambitious achievers and more than its share of swindlers and conmen. Somehow they all managed to find a place in the cultural circus of California, as do those who arrive as casual visitors and never leave.

# *I*NTRODUCTION

## History and Population

For thousands of years, various Indian tribes found a foothold within every niche of California's diverse environment. In 1542, Juan Rodriguez Cabrillo, a Portuguese seaman in the service of Spain, set forth to explore the completely unknown coast north of Mexico, and to claim any lands possible for Spain. Cabrillo's expedition set out because of the Spanish empire's desire for expansion in the New World. It really was a new world, promising endless riches, but vastness and mystery as well. Only 50 years had passed since Columbus discovered America, and less than 25 since Cortes had vanquished Aztec Mexico. Cabrillo himself had marched with the famed *conquistador*. Mexico brimmed with rumors of vast fortunes piled in the northern hinterland. Antonio de Mendoza, Viceroy of Mexico and rival of Cortez for power, had only two years earlier dispatched Francisco Coronado to seek the fabled Seven Cities of Cibola in the region of New Mexico. Now he sent out Cabrillo, a skilled navigator, determined to break through the known limits of the earth. His quest was inspired by the legend of an island kingdom whose huge warriors carried swords of gold, as well as by hopes of discovering a secret passage to the Orient.

Cabrillo set sail in June with two small ships from the Mexican port of Navidad, and reached San Diego Bay in late September. He pushed northward along the coast, observing the plains and mountains of the interior, toward the island of **Santa Catalina**. He named the landmarks he passed (most of the names have been forgotten today) and claimed each for the King of Spain. His ships hugged the coast, trailed by Indians in canoes eager to barter.

In November, Cabrillo landed in the Channel Island archipelago, probably on **San Miguel Island**. As he rushed to help some soldiers who were scuffling with Indians ashore, he fell and broke a leg. Infection set in, and Cabrillo's condition deteriorated over the next six weeks. Amazingly, he retained command and steered his ships north through battering storms off the coast of **Big Sur**.

Cabrillo sailed northward as far as present-day **Fort Ross**, then returned to what was probably San Miguel Island where he finally died and was buried. His grave has not been found. Under the chief pilot, the expedition continued as far north as southern Oregon before it finally returned south.

The expedition reached Navidad in April, 1543, ten months after it departed. It brought back a wealth of information about the bays, inlets, natives and rich potential of the northern coast, and made claims to California for Spain that were not challenged for almost three hundred years. However, it found no golden swords, or passage to China, and it left behind the remains of an intrepid explorer.

Cabrillo's exploration of the Pacific Coast opened California to the

# *I*NTRODUCTION

European world, but there was little settlement on the part of the Spanish or anyone else. In 1579 Sir Francis Drake claimed the **San Francisco** area for the Queen of England. Various explorers made forays along the coast, but it was only when the Russians began to move down from Alaska and establish hunting and trading outposts as far south as the Sonoma coast, that the Spanish began to initiate settlement.

The first settlement was established in 1769 in **San Diego**, as a joint military-religious enterprise, with Father Junipero Serra overseeing the construction of a mission intended for the conversion of the local Indians. San Diego was the first of a chain of missions which Serra built, in an effort which was continued by others after his death.

A mission often appeared first with a presidio, and only later did a pueblo — a secular civilian settlement — grow near it. This was a common pattern. The San Gabriel Mission, for example, established in 1771, provided the impetus for the construction of a small village nine miles away, called **Los Angeles**.

The missions were all built along the coast, about a day's journey apart. The paths and dirt roads worn between the missions were eventually spliced into a main coastal road, called El Camino Real, still marked by roadside signs today.

The padres of the far-flung Franciscan missions were immersed as much in physical labor as in spiritual. They were pioneers and settlers, as well as padres. It must have been an amazing time to be in California; everything was new, untouched, open, and the surrounding land so deeply beautiful.

The missions prospered. The padres tilled the fertile valleys. They planted grain crops as well as olives, figs, grape vines, and fruits and vegetables from Spain and Mexico. Their large herds of livestock grazed in the virgin grasslands. In some missions the padres built sophisticated and extensive water systems. The tracts under Franciscan ownership and tillage were immense. By the time the last mission was completed in 1823, the missions controlled one sixth of the total land in California.

But much of this physical progress rested on the backs of local Indians. Conversion was massive and rapid. Many Indians drew toward the missions and the new way of life, while others were pressed into service. There were many forced conversions, resulting in rebellion and consequent repression and punishment. The urge to hasten the Indians' enlightenment might have been intensified if they happened to dwell upon a particularly fertile stretch of land. About 2,000 Chumash Indians were removed en masse from Santa Cruz Island to the Santa Barbara mission.

Written testimony from the early 19th century details regular whippings of Indians in some missions. Even the much-praised

Father Serra was reprimanded by the Spanish governor for implementing excessively heavy punishments. Moreover, the changing of age-old life patterns and sexual molestation by local soldiers, exposed the mission Indians to epidemics. In the sixty years of Spanish control, the Indian population in those areas dropped from about 130 thousand to 83 thousand, with a much higher death rate among the mission Indians.

Rebellion in the 1820's was anti-clerical as well as anti-Spanish. With independence won in 1833, the Mexican congress wrested the missions from Franciscan control. The missions were secularized and stripped of their vast tracts of land. They went into decline, and some into deep decay. Various parties found ways to claim title to land parcels. Later, some of the missions were restored and returned to Franciscan auspices.

The missions left a legacy for Mexican and American rule. They were the first to experiment with California's tremendous agricultural potential. They bequeathed a style of architecture harmonious with the landscape, and several mission names now belong to major cities. The missions gave local Indians new skills for the new world that was fast approaching. They also reduced and deeply scarred the Indian population, but that was but a prelude to future actions. A fiew dacades later, when Mexico won her independence from Spain in 1882 and California was not Mexican anymore, the missions were secularized and efforts were made to expand and solidify settlement.

Meanwhile, an increasing number of American settlers and sailors moved into California. By the mid-1840s there was a call in the east for the annexation of California, as part of the American philosophy of "Manifest Destiny"; the establishment of a republic from coast to coast. In 1848 the mexican war, between Mexico and U.S., came to its end after three years of fighting. One of its consequences — California was ceded to the U.S.

At this year of its turnover to the United States, gold was discovered in California in the Sierra foothills of **Sutter's Mill**. Within a few years the population escalated by about 1000%, and California became the main attraction for American settlers who dreamed of striking it rich.

Gold-hungry immigrants used the local Indian population to work the mines. The Indians were enormously abused. California historian Josian Royce describes how some miners used Indian villages as "targets for rifle-practice, or to destroy wholesale with fire, outrage and murder, as if they had been so many wasps' nests in our gardens at home". The 100,000 Indians in California in 1846 were reduced to 31,000 by 1852. Those left were humiliated, uprooted and exposed to epidemic diseases and alcohol. Over 7 million acres were left to the California Indians by signed treaty in 1850, but this was whittled down to a pitiful 500,000 acres. It was only in 1963 that the California Indians were awarded $27 million by the federal government as long overdue compensation for the lands they lost.

After the Civil War, the national economy and industry boomed, and in 1869 California was linked to the east by the first trans-continental railroad.

California's history has been a record of booms and depressions; of land sales, land grabs and land frauds; of the discovery of new resources and the sudden influx of people to exploit them. The discovery of oil in **Los Angeles** and **Long Beach** at the end of the 19th century created an economic boom in Los Angeles.

With the creation of the movie industry in Hollywood, a new kind of wealth was created in California, and there was suddenly a large number of self-made millionaires. A glamorous "royalty" of movie stars was created, and in their wake thousands of hopefuls flocked to Los Angeles seeking glory in celluloid, but finding instead jobs as cooks, waitresses and cops.

During the Great Depression, more hordes crossed the eastern hills into the valleys seeking not fame and fortune but work, bread or a little land. With this influx of "Oakies" came an ideological clash between radicalism and conservative, land-holding interests. Labor protests, which were violently supressed, burst forth everywhere.

In the 1940s fear of the Japanese replaced fear of the "Reds". In anticipation of the Japanese invasion that never came, thousands of American citizens of Japanese descent were interned in isolated camps, and much of their property was confiscated or looted.

In the 1950s post-war prosperity, the attraction of California became even stronger. The aeronautics industry drew thousands of workers and became the state's industrial and technological mainstay, which it remained until the recent surge in microelectronics took hold in the **Silicon Valley** (at **San Jose**) and revolutionized technology. A steady stream of residents still flows to California. By 1964, California had surpassed New York as the country's most populous state, and today the population exceeds 25 million.

People are attracted to the "sunbelt" of the west and southwest, including an influx of foreign immigrants. California has always attracted a variety of ethnic groups with its multitudinous economic opportunities. Today's immigrants do not come from European countries, but from the Pacific areas and Latin America.

California has been in flux from the moment of statehood. For over a hundred years, the population doubled every twenty years. Although that rate has slowed slightly, the change in the ethnic fabric of the state has accelerated. In the last 15 years, the percentage of Hispanics has almost doubled and the percentage of Asians has almost tripled, while the Caucasian population has dropped considerably. Immigration is becoming one of the key issues of California's future as, in a sense, it has been for over 150 years. The number of children growing up speaking a first language other than English is rapidly growing, yet English has been voted as the single official language of the state.

Meanwhile California's breakneck development and technological advancement continues, swelling its population, taking over rich farmland and exploiting natural resources. Some demographers predict that the population could reach 35 million by the year 2000. Whatever the future holds, no doubt California will face it in its typically dynamic, experimental and completely individual way.

## Geography

The coast of California is about 900 miles (1440 km) long, from **Crescent City** at the Oregan border to **San Diego** at the Mexican border. The north coast has endless acres of tall pines and redwoods. The coast is rocky and studded with cliffs, and just beyond the beach area there are ranges of coastal mountains.

The mountain ranges stretch east, reaching towering Mt. Shasta at the southern tip of the Cascade Mountains. Beyond the Cascades, in the northeastern corner of the state, is a strange, weathered and pockmarked world of ancient lava. Below this mountainous cap, which spans the width of California, many of the state's topographical features run parallel to the coast.

Along the northern border, down past the Golden Gate and **San Francisco**, past **Monterey Bay** to the cliffs of **Big Sur**, the coast is stark, and the weather is foggy due to cold currents. Further south, however, near **Santa Barbara**, the ocean currents are warm, and the weather is gentler. The beaches are also softer. The land becomes drier and scrubbier towards the Los Angeles basin which is surrounded by mountains. South of this point the land basks in a hot, constant, semi-tropical sun.

A range of hills runs along the coast from the north, almost all the way down to Mexico. They extend towards the east and in the central part of the state, reach into the rich San Joaquin Valley. This valley is a 400-mile (640 km) long fertile furrow running through the heart of the state. It stretches from the foot of the Cascades in the north, (as the Sacramento Valley), past **Sacramento** to **Bakersfield**, stopping before the thin barrier of the Tehachapi range that separates it from Los Angeles. This great valley is paralled on the east by the long granite massif of the **Sierra Nevada**. The mountain slopes rise gently from the west, in round compact hills where the discovery of gold launched the mad rush of the 1850s. The sequoia trees, the largest living things on earth, grow higher up on the slopes of these hills.

# *I*NTRODUCTION

Numerous westward-flowing rivers, with the assistance of ancient glaciers, carved the cliffs, domes and cascades of the Yosemite Valley and other canyons. Yosemite National Park, Lake Tahoe, and King's Canyon/Sequoia National Parks are the main sights of the Sierras. Through the whole range runs a majestic spine of craggy and snow-covered peaks, which is superb backpacking country.

The eastern slope drops like a sheer granite wall, into a high semi arid plateau. This is the great Basin, with isolated mountain peaks, alkaline flats and ancient bristlecone pines 4,000 years old. The Basin extends as far as the desert.

The desert forms the state's largest geographical entity. East of the Sierras, it extends south towards Mexico and stretches across the border. In the east, it extends to the Colorado River and into Nevada and Arizona, and in the west towards Los Angeles.

## Climate

The climate in California varies greatly according to the region. In the south, the summers are hot and dry and the sun shines most of the year. The rains usually come in winter, though interspersed with sunshine. Near the beaches especially, it may be tempered by refreshing breezes, but summer in the L.A. urban area can also bring on smog alerts, when the sky is hazy not from fog but from the brown clouds of pollution, and venturing forth in such conditions can actually be hazardous. Winter temperatures of 40 degrees Fahrenheit (4.5 degrees Centigrade) are considered cold enough here to wear minks and down jackets.

The deserts can be comfortable during most of the year but broiling in the summer. The dry heat, however, is more bearable than humidity. Desert summer nights are warm and comfortable, but temperatures can sometimes drop sharply at sunset. An occasional summer rain in the desert is a welcome relief. The clouds swirl and gleam, and the rain churns up delicious fresh smells from the desert floor. In winter the desert can be quite windy and cold.

Seasons in the California mountains are more sharply demarcated than along the coast. Summers can be hot, punctuated by rains, and summer evenings can turn breezy and cool. In the immense areas of conifers, autumn can barely be distinguished, but in some areas where deciduous trees follow the course of stream, the autumnal mountains are etched with rivers of blazing gold.

The first snows can fall as early as late September, and they fall not only in soft white flutterings but in full-fledged blizzards. Snow can pile up to 20 feet (7 m) or more, and last well into spring. In the mountains in late spring the many streams are turbulent and swollen with melted snow.

In the San Joaquin Valley, the summer heat is humid, and extremely unpleasant. That's when you'll want to press your foot on the accelerator and buzz along that super-highway as fast as possible.

Northern California, along the coast, is characterised by wet winters, often with very heavy rainfall. Nevertheless, there are plenty of fresh and blue-skied winter days as well. The summers can be cool, foggy and overcast, but generally not for long durations. Inland, the winters are a bit drier.

## California Literature

California, as a physical reality and state of mind, has attracted both American and foreign writers since before the Gold Rush days. A number of books will give you a feel for the unique texture of California.

Raymond Chandler, mysteries: Corruption and murder in a young Los Angeles, as seen through the eyes of private eye Philip Marlowe.

Richard Henry Dana, *Two Years Before the Mast*: A vivid and detailed travelogue in the 19th-century tradition. With tremendous accuracy he describes the coast of what was then a new and wide-open world.

Joan Didion, *Slouching Towards Bethlehem*: Well-known essays on modern California life and manners.

Allen Ginsberg, *Howl*: Ginsberg's unleashing of this powerful poem became a literary turning point in San Francisco. With Jack Kerouac he helped create a literary movement.

Dashiell Hammett, mysteries: The San Francisco bars frequented by his hard-boiled detective Sam Spade still stand today. Hammett's tough and laconic style greatly influenced many other mystery writers, particularly Raymond Chandler.

Bret Hart, *The Outcast of Poker Flat*: An American story writer and journalist, Hart was the first to depict life in the gold-mining days.

Robinson Jeffers, poetry: Jeffers spent years on the Big Sur coast, and uses the cliffs and waves as powerful metaphors.

Jack Kerouac, *On the Road*: This, the most sincere of Kerouac's writing, preached a "spontaneous" way of life. This work helped launch the beatnik generation.

Henry Miller, *Big Sur and the Oranges of Hieronymous Bosch*: After exploring the alleys and brothels of Paris, Miller stumbled into the wild coast where he found a sense of peace and a focus for his prose.

John Muir, various writings. Elegant descriptions of nature and the wilderness.

John Steinbeck, *The Grapes of Wrath, Of Mice and Men, East of Eden, Cannery Row, Tortilla Flat, In Dubious Battle*: The *Grapes of Wrath* is Steinbeck's masterpiece about the odyssey of a migrant family to the farmlands of California. Virtually all of his best writing concerns California. No one writes of the state, and its less shining characters, with more wisdom, warmth and compassion.

Mark Twain, *Roughing It*: No one is more hilarious, or shrewdly observant in capturing the frontier and the Gold Rush.

Evelyn Waugh, *The Loved One*: A biting satire on the American undertaking industry, based around a gaudy and pretentious Los Angeles cemetery.

## Pop Architecture

Weird and wonderful architectural forms are as much a part of California's heritage as the rambling Victorian buildings and stucco cottages with red tile roofs. Giant donuts, ice cream cones, owls and hearts, big hats and tractors, towering cowboys, lumberjacks and dinosaurs decorate the California landscape.

Imaginative architecture, which served as advertising, sprang up in the 1920s, with the advent of the automobile, a growing highway system and a newly-mobile middle class. Even during the Depression years, such building continued. It became the expression of hundreds of small private dreams and fantasies.

California soil seemed fertile for such imaginative advertising. Space was wide open, land was available, and already the state was becoming based on the automobile. There was relatively little existing architectural tradition, and the commercial and imaginative climate was right for a bit of profitable whimsy. Any commercial gimmick that might turn a buck had a fighting chance in California. You might say that scattered along the highways of southern California were the precursors of Disneyland. Igloos and castles, southern manors and quaint thatched-roof villages became landmarks. The *Tail o' the Pup*, on the 300 block of La Cienega in Los Angeles, was clever play on the word "hot dog". An L. A. institution, it has appeared in many movies including the relatively recent *Ruthless People*. In Castroville, during a public-relations effort to get the local artichokes on the map, a 16-foot (5 m) artichoke, complete with spikes, was planted in the ground.

The king of pop art architecture in California must be *Dinny the Dinosaur*, at the Cabazon exit off I-10 on the way to Palm Springs. It is the creation of Claude Bell, who was inspired as a boy by a giant elephant-shaped hotel in the New Jersey resort of Margate. He designed many sculptures and buildings for fairs and parks.

When he moved to California and bought a desert plot on which he opened a restaurant, his dream evolved in the shape of a brontosaurus three times the size of a real one! Dinny was a labor of love that took ten years to build. His belly houses a museum and small apartment, reached by a stairway through the tail. He surpasses other roadside models not only in size but through the graceful proportions and meticulous detail, down to the wrinkles and lumps in his hide. Bell was still busy working on his primeval pets into his nineties, having added a tyrannosaurus (with a viewing platform on its head and a slide down its back) to keep Dinny company. The two prehistoric reptiles are clearly visible from the highway and look poised to gobble up the trucks lined up outside the restaurant.

# *I*NTRODUCTION

# Part Two — Setting Out

## How to get there

**By air:** The two major airports in California are **Los Angeles International Airport (LAX)** and the **San Francisco Airport (SFO)**. Both airports are served by major international and domestic airlines. San Diego airport also serves an increasing amount of national and international air traffic. Special offers of air tickets are worth investigating.

**By land:** Main train routes to California run from Seattle to San Francisco, Chicago to San Francisco and Chicago to Los Angeles. Major bus companies are *Greyhound* and *Trailways*, which both have special offers and various travel options. Car rental is probably the best way of getting around California.

## Documents and customs regulations

### Visas
Foreign visitors must enter the United States with a valid passport and visa. Most B-2 tourist visas are valid for 6 months. A lost visa can be replaced through the embassy of the visitor's country. To apply for a visa extension, or to replace the arrival/departure form received on arrival, a foreign citizen must go to the nearest U.S. Immigration and Naturalization Service office.

If you have any problems, it is advisable to contact the nearest consulate of your country. Many countries have consular offices in Los Angeles and/or San Francisco.

A foreign visitor can bring in $100 worth of gifts into the U.S. duty-free, up to 200 cigarettes, and a liter of alcohol. There is no limit on currency. Prescription drugs should be clearly visible and labeled, accompanied by a copy of the doctor's prescription.

### International Driver's License
A driver's license valid for the U.S. should be obtained in the country of origin. It will not be issued in the U.S.

### Student Cards
Students with proper identification can often receive considerable

discount on transportation fares, hotel rates and admission prices. Proper identification includes either a valid university identification card, or an **International Student Identity Card (ISIC)**. The latter, which costs $8, can be obtained with proof of full-time student status. This could be a university identification card, a stamped letter from the registrar, a current grade report, etc. Students enrolled at school for the previous fall semester are eligible to receive the card. In certain cities, with junior colleges, full-time registration costs are negligible, and people have been known to register for a semester just to obtain a student card.

The Council of International Educational Exchange (CIEE) sponsors a special discount plan which, for a small sum, entitles the holder to 25% savings on room rates at various lodgings. Much additional advice on travel is available. To use these services, an ISIC is required, and is obtainable from the CIEE.

### Insurance

Insurance is essential. Do not play games with health or medical emergency, even though most major centers do have crisis centers or public clinics that can and will offer immediate care to the uninsured. University hospitals will often do the same. Call the local emergency number, or the crisis center mentioned in this book.

The insuring of valuable objects, such as cameras, is obviously a personal choice. In the big cities especially, professional thieves abound and are very smooth. This is not meant to frighten you off, but it is best to be realistic. A moment's carelessness, a camera can disappear. Insurance can sometimes be purchased through a travel organization.

## Safety Precautions

It is best to avoid bus terminals and train stations late at night, and it is not advisable to walk in deserted downtown neighborhoods at high. Avoid public restrooms in the cities.

It is advisable to keep some money separate from your wallet, and to keep a list of traveler's checks separate as well. Make a note of important numbers — driver's license, credit card, passport — and keep it somewhere safe.

Many travelers choose to carry money and important documents in a money belt that fits around the waist inside the shirt, or one that hangs around the neck. Some go so far as to carry a "decoy" wallet in a pocket, to draw attention away from the money belt. All this is a matter of personal choice. The most important thing is to take the steps necessary for your own peace of mind and maximum enjoyment.

## When to come; National Holidays

California is a vacationland for all seasons. During every season of the year, there is at least one part of the state where the weather seems just perfect.

Most people flock to California in the summer, and in most tourist areas prices tend to rise accordingly. The exception to this is the desert resort of Palm Springs where prices actually go down in summer due to the intense heat. Winters in southern California are delightfully sunny and warm; summers in northern California are refreshingly cool. In the Sierra Nevada and the other mountain ranges, each season has its own beauty and activities. Some mountain passes are closed in winter, but the mountain ski resorts are popular.

Planning a time for your visit may be not so much a matter of weather, but rather a matter of crowds. There is no doubt that most tourist facilities are far more crowded in summer, with a commensurate rise in prices. If possible, try and avoid traveling on the following days:

Memorial Day weekend, around May 31st.
Independence Day weekend, around July 4th.
Labor Day weekend, at the beginning of September.

From Memorial Day onwards, there is a great increase in the number of vacationers on the roads, with a sharp decline following Labor Day. In fact, in terms of numbers, prices, and the accessibility of facilities, early fall is an ideal time to travel. Children are back at school and students are back at college.

The weeks surrounding Christmas and New Year's Day are also crowded with visitors. However, the rest of the winter is considered off-season, other than for ski resorts.

American public holidays include:
New Year's Day, January 1st.
President's Day, the third Monday in February.
Memorial Day, the last Monday in May.
Independence Day, July 4th (businesses close on the nearest Monday or Friday).
Labor Day, first Monday in September.
Columbus Day, second Monday in October.
Veteran's Day, November 11th.
Thanksgiving, last Thursday in November.
Christmas, December 25th.

## What to wear

Clothing to be packed depends upon the region to be visited. For southern California, be sure to pack a heavy sweater and light waterproof coat for the winter. You will need these in summer in northern California. Style in California tends to be casual.

Ties are usually worn by businessmen, but this is not as strictly required as it is in the east. Colors for both men's and women's fashions are brighter in California than in some other regions, and also brighter in the south than in the north. Californian casualness has become a fashion in its own right, blending a bright, tailored tapered look with comfort. Shoes can also be casual. A good pair of walking shoes can serve in a number of situations. There always seems to be a sale at one or another of the numerous clothing stores, so it is easy to pick up what you need. For women, slacks are acceptable for most occasions, and are worn by many.

California is also the place for down-to-earth second-hand artistic funk. "Contemporary Salvation Army" is becoming so popular that charity and second-hand stores have begun to raise their prices, and some have turned downright chic.

If planning to enjoy California's natural wonders, be sure to include sturdy durable clothes and shoes. In southern California especially, a hat, preferably broad-brimmed, is advisable during the summer. Sandals are increasingly accepted as everyday summer footwear. Birkenstocks, though more expensive than some others, are sturdy, long-lasting, comfortable and popular. For hiking shoes, the new models made of light yet water resistant material, are gaining in popularity. These are suitable for California's diverse terrains.

## How much will it cost

The amount of money a visitor will spend is, of course, a very subjective matter, depending on the individual's needs, tastes and style. The point to remember is that California, more than many other areas, provides enough variety in resources and alternatives for most people to relax and enjoy themselves within their means.

The main expense, besides the cost of getting to California, will naturally be **lodging**. The prices of average lodging has sky-rocketed in recent years. Even Motel 6, which made its name an advertisement of its price, would have to change its name to Motel 21.50 to be accurate today. For a standard basic motel room, expect to pay a minimum of $23-$30 per day. Most cost considerably more. For an average motel room or a room in a B&B a visitor could easily pay $50-$60 per day. Of course there are plenty of better hotels that charge up to $150 per day for their amenities; spending more is never a problem.

# *I*NTRODUCTION

Nevertheless, a person on a strict budget can definitely find cheap accommodation, and in some comfort, if he or she shows some flexibility. Hostels, for example, though not the last word in luxury or privacy, rarely cost more than $8 per day, and provide a unique traveling experience. YMCAs offer another inexpensive solution. The person determined to backpack can do so and still have access to the major cities. Car-camping is popular, and private and public campgrounds are numerous, ranging between $6-$15 per night, depending on the place, facilities, etc.

**Transportation** costs can also vary greatly. Car-rental can range from $20-$40 per day. Insurance is added on a daily basis (see "Car Rental"). Local bus systems may cost between 50 cents and $1, usually with some sort of transfer arrangement. Transportation between major cities is private. Buses cost approximately $14 between Los Angeles and San Diego, and $25-$40 between Los Angeles and San Francisco. Private vans, airport shuttles and so forth can start at about $7 and go up to $20.

Those preferring to work on a firm transportation budget may want to base costs on monthly car rentals ($400 and up, plus insurance), or monthly bus or train passes. These can be combined with local public transportation, daily car or bicycle rental (see "Transportation").

As for **food**, there is a wide range of budgeting possibilities, especially in the two major urban areas, where the choice and variety is enormous. Cheapest of all is to buy from grocery stores, delis and fast-food stands, but a good and filling meal in certain restaurants can be had for as little as $3-$5. Good breakfasts can cost from $1.50-$3.50. Many places, especially simple Chinese restaurants, have lunch specials costing $3-$5. Mexican restaurants cost slightly more, with large meals running from $4.50-$6. Salad bars start at about $3.50 and up.

Steak or fish meals in good restaurants start at about $10, but the same meal, during an "Early Bird Special" will cost about $6.95. (There is almost no upper limit.) At the lower limit, even a really inexpensive special will cost about $5, including beverage and tip.

California, especially southern California, is a shopper's and bargain-seeker's paradise. Discount houses proliferate and large drug-store chains sell merchandise at cut-rate prices.

**Entertainment** — night clubs, concerts and shows — can be expensive. Many clubs include a cover charge and a one or two-drink minimum. For a couple, that could reach approximately $20. First run movies cost about $5-6. Such attractions as amusement parks are especially expensive. Admission for some of these private tourist attractions is over $10 per person, with a parking fee slapped on top.

On the other hand, some of the top museums in the country are

# *I**NTRODUCTION*

found in California, and are open to the public for nominal prices. Many museums, as mentioned throughout the book, set aside special hours or days when admission is free.

# $I$NTRODUCTION

# Part Three — Easing the Shock: Where Have We Landed?

## Transportation

### Airports

The two major airports in California are the **Los Angeles (LAX)** and the **San Francisco (SFO)** airports. LAX is one of the busiest in the world. All major domestic and just about all major international and foreign lines serve the two airports. There is also an extremely busy commuter lane between SFO and LAX, in addition to numerous flights taking off to and from smaller airports within the same corridor.

The **San Diego** airport (SAN) also services flights along the coast and handles an increasing amount of national and international traffic.

There are several airlines that operate mainly in the west, and others that operate solely within California. It is possible to fly all around the state with small airlines such as Pacific Coast, Sky West, Mid Pacific, as well as on larger regional airlines such as PSA or Western. A number of smaller metropolitan airports handle major national carriers. This not only reduces the strain on the major airports, but allows the visitor greater flexibility. During high-season or on busy holiday weekends, it is sometimes wise to avoid a major center such as LAX and rather to land in a less frenetic local airport. The possibilities for direct air connections to the lesser-known areas of California are often much greater than visitors realize.

The following airports handle national airlines:
Arcata/Eureka: tel.707-445-7791.
Bakersfield (Meadows Field): tel. 805-393-7977.
Burbank-Glendale-Pasadena: tel. 818-840-8843.
Fresno: tel. 251-6051.
Long Beach: tel. 213-421-8293.
Los Angeles: tel. 213-646-5252 (also for international flights).
Monterey Peninsula: tel. 408-373-3731.
Oakland: tel. 415-577-4000 (also international flights).
Ontario: tel. 714-984-1207 (also international flights).
Palm Springs: tel. 619-323-8163.
Reno: tel. 702-785-2575.
Sacramento: tel. 916-929-5411.

San Francisco: tel. 415-761-0800 (also international flights).
San Diego: tel. 619-231-5220 (also international flights).
San Jose: tel. 408-277-5366.
Santa Barbara: tel. 805-967-1613 or 805-967-7111.

Since the deregulation of the airline industry a few years ago, and with new companies springing up and competition growing intense, the air traveler has been benefiting. If you shop around and are a bit flexible with your flying schedule, you can find some amazing flight deals, especially compared with what passengers paid some years back. Of course this could change. The airline industry, at least in America, is in great flux, but right now it is a flier's market.

When booking a flight, do not settle for the first answer you get, from either an airline or a travel agent. Try other airlines and other agents, until you have a good idea of the price range.

It might be up to you to ask the pertinent questions. Sometimes you must ferret out the details: they will not always be volunteered. Are there student fares? Stand-by fares? Midnight fares? Does a round-trip bought in advance cost less? Would the price be lower during another season? Airline officials often cannot answer all your questions because they do not know. With some special flight bargains, however, the deal comes with restrictions which will be made clear to you.

If you have purchased a round-trip ticket to the United States from abroad (some companies may require foreign residency), then you can buy a **VUSA** (Visit USA) ticket. This allows you to fly literally all over the United States for one set price — generally between $200-$400 — which is usually less than one standard cross-country flight. There are several similar types of VUSA tickets, based on a system whereby you pay a set price, and take an unlimited number of flights with the airline issuing the ticket, within a specific time limit. The only restriction is that you cannot leave from or enter the same terminal more than twice.

Even if you plan to stay within one region, such as California or the West Coast, a VUSA might still be worthwhile, as it may cost the same as one standard flight from the East Coast. Furthermore, some regional airlines have arrangements which honor the VUSA ticket of certain major airlines. If, for example, you buy a VUSA from Northwest Airlines, you can use it on PSA all through California and the West with no extra charge. Check this out, because the arrangements can change periodically.

Many airlines have introduced, to the travelers' delight, a variety of **Frequent-Flyers** programs, in which the miles you fly can be used as credit toward free future flights. Business person who travel frequently can clock up enormous amounts of free mileage. The system is generally based on miles flown. Check these plans carefully, because with some companies you are given points only for the number of flights, regardless of the mileage of each flight. PSA seems to have the best frequent-flyer program in the West, more advantageous than that of Western, its major competitor.

There is also the new, unofficial "bumping game" that has taken over the airlines. Airlines now make a practice of overbooking certain, generally crowded, flights, to compensate for the number of people who make reservations and who do not turn up. If most or all passengers show up, however, then the airlines have more people than seats. Thanks to the efforts of consumer advocate Ralph Nader (after he himself was ignominiously "bumped" from an overbooked plane), government regulations require that passengers bumped involuntarily must be given cash payments, sometimes double the cost of the ticket; and they can still sue.

Financially ailing airlines, to avoid having to fork out cash, have come up with another solution. They ask for volunteers to give up their seat, and offer free tickets to various destinations in addition to a guaranteed seat on the next flight. This has become so commonplace that people make a sport of it. They've learned the angles and purposely book themselves on busy flights, their hands ready to shoot up the moment volunteers are requested. Businessmen have become pros. You may not be in their champion class, but if your schedule is flexible, the wrong flight may turn into the right flight, resulting in a voucher for a free trip somewhere.

**Trains**: Train travel is a throwback to a bygone world. The conductor rattles off the names of exotic-sounding frontier towns. The train pulls into an elegant Spanish-style station, or past a small smudged brick depot bordered by decrepit hotels and bars. People casually get acquainted in the lounge car. The countryside glides by at eye-level. The traveling becomes as rich an experience as the arrival.

*Amtrak*, the national passenger rail carrier, made a big push recently to encourage train travel by introducing extended routes, lower rates, package-tour deals, streamlined equipment and so forth. All this is geared to fill their trains, which were, for a while, pitifully empty.

The main train routes leading into California include:
Seattle to San Francisco (The Coast Starlight).
Chicago to San Francisco (The California Zephyr).
Chicago to Los Angeles, either directly through San Antonio, or through New Orleans (The Desert Wind).

An intricate system of buses and local commuter trains connects with *Amtrak* rail lines, greatly extending access by train.

There are several main routes within the state. The **Coast Starlight** takes ten-and-a+half hours between Los Angeles and San Francisco. This route affords a slow but pleasant way to travel between the major cities without the hassles of driving. Although it does not follow the rugged Big Sur Coast, the train passes some gorgeous shoreline.

In the San Francisco area, the actual departure station is in industrial Oakland. A special *Amtrak* bus connects to the San Francisco station, the trans-bay terminal, at 1st and Mission.

The California section of the **Zephyr** follows the route of the early transcontinental railroad, with access to the Truckee-Lake Tahoe area, as well as to Reno just across the Sierra Nevada.

The San Joaquin route runs through the main cities of the Central Valley. From Bakersfield in the south, a special *Amtrak* bus brings passengers to the *Amtrak* station in the Los Angeles area. In the north, the train connects with the main east-west line and with the train going north to Seattle. At various points along this route, there are connections with local and regional bus lines. At the **Merced** station, a private bus runs to Yosemite Park.

At the time of writing, *Amtrak* has a special scheme whereby for any regular ticket purchase of $60 or more, the return fare is only $7. In California, even some routes with fares less than $60 qualify for the special return fare, such as the routes between Los Angeles and San Diego, and between San Francisco and Bakersfield. You need to return by the same route, and there are no stopovers. The $7 fare is good for 45 days after the original trip. There are certain peak traveling seasons when the ticket is not valid, so check this out carefully.

*Amtrak* also has special fares for traveling within or between various regions of the country. If you are journeying to California from the east, a $250 fare allows you to weave towards the west along whatever route you want, with three stopovers within 45 days. Coming from the mid-west, the fare is $200. To zig-zag throughout the western region, from El Paso, Texas to Spokane, Washington including all of California, costs $150. As with the airlines, *Amtrak's* offers change often, so it is important to call for updated information.

*Amtrak* also offers total travel packages with hotels, tours, etc. There are such tours for Hearst Castle, the wine country, San Francisco and Disneyland. Trains have sleeping accommodation, ranging from a pillow for the seat to separate bedrooms, complete with bathroom. Some trains — or specific types of cars — require reservations, while others do not. If you buy your ticket on the train, when the station booth is open, you will be required to pay an additional $3. It is possible to bring bicycles aboard certain trains, without have to dismantle the bikes. For general *Amtrak* information and reservations: tel. 1-800-872-7245. This number will give you various local *Amtrak* numbers, if needed.

# *I*NTRODUCTION

## Buses

The two major private bus companies are *Greyhound* and *Trailways*. Both companies offer special excursion fares, summer-travel fares and so forth. As with *Amtrak*, these rates and schedules change often, so it is always worth double-checking. *Greyhound* with its *Ameripass*, and Trailways with its *Eaglepass*, both offer unlimited travel for a fixed price, within a fixed number of days. Although most buses are stream-lined and comfortable, there is a limit to how long you can remain seated, especially when you push yourself, because you want to get the most for your money. Compare prices with *Amtrak*. In some cases, surprisingly, the train's bargain pass may actually be cheaper, and they are certainly more comfortable. For those wanting to reach California cheaply, both bus companies offer a 15-day one-way fare, in which travel in one direction for up to 15 days costs about $100. Stops are permitted.

Children between 12-16 ride for half-fare, and ages 11 and under ride free. Seniors receive a 10% discount except on special fares. Bicycles can be stowed in the baggage compartment. This opens the possibility for a hop-scotch travel schedule of bus rides and bike rides.

Bus stations almost always seem to be located in the bad part of town. If possible, avoid arriving late at night or having to wait around a dingy and depressing bus station in the wee hours.

*Green Tortoise* buses offer alternative tours which are adventurous (slightly), eccentric and cheap. The company once had a reputation as the "freak" bus line, but now it draws a wide variety of people, from hippies to foreigners to professionals and spunky seniors seeking an unusual travel experience. The buses have bunks (bring your own sleeping bag or bedding), and two drivers to allow night-time traveling and daytime excursions and diversions. For the lone traveler with a budget one notch above hitching, *Green Tortoise* provides a chance to meet similar travelers, to make contacts, to pick up traveling tips and just to have some company.

*Green Tortoise* conducts trips to Alaska, Vancouver and cross-country tours varying in duration and routes (one tour hits the major national parks). A cross-country to California costs about $200. There is also a strong schedule within California, including $25 trips between San Francisco and Los Angeles with stops for exploring. There are also trips to Yosemite ($49-$59). Communally-cooked vegetarian meals fuel the crew and the travelers. Each bus has a stereo, and you can volunteer your own cassettes.

*Green Tortoise* Main office: P.O.Box 24459, San Francisco, 94124. tel.415-821-0803. There are offices on the east coast and along the west coast, and a toll-free number, tel. 1-800-277-4766.

# *I*NTRODUCTION

## Car Rental

Renting a car can be the most convenient and the most expensive means of travel in California. It is worth calling up several agencies because rates and conditions vary widely. For a day, a car could cost from $16-$30, and per month between $450-$550. The larger agencies — *Hertz, Avis* and *National* — are available at airports and major tourist centers, but do not necessarily offer the best deals. Sometimes, the small agencies boast the best prices. Most major California cities have the equivalent of "rent-a+wreck" car rentals, giving just what the name applies, at commensurate prices, along with a certain distance radius.

3,000 miles (4,800 km) a month — the average amount given — may seem like sufficient distance, but that breaks down to just over one hundred miles per day, which, if you are a hard-pushing traveler, is not really very much. Los Angeles commuters easily cover that distance daily.

The real drawback to renting a car can be the insurance, which may cost $6-$8 per day. You can apply your own liability insurance, but only if you are an in-state driver with a California license. Of course, in that case there is less chance you would need to rent a car: one of life's little ironies. If you are entering California from outside the state and want to rent a car, you almost have no choice but to take the insurance as well. Some agencies might advise you to attach yourself to the insurance of a relative, but be very wary of this as it stands on shaky legal ground. When inquiring about the insurance, find out exactly what is covered. Agents have been known to quote insurance prices, only to reveal later that the coverage is only partial, and they then try to convince you to take on "extra" protection ("Perhaps you'd like your left tires covered as well?").

The larger agencies sometimes offer special weekend rates. These can start as early as Thursday, with a package deal for rental through Sunday.

Having access to a car makes all the difference in the world, especially in southern California. For both the business traveler on a strict schedule, and the tourist, it may be best to fly between destinations and rent cars locally. California's excellent in-state and inter-region air connections allows this to be done with flexibility and ease.

A **drive-away** company offers a slightly uncertain but inexpensive way to travel, both to California and within the state. These companies find drivers to transport cars from one destination to another. It is usually easy to find cars being transported from coast to coast. Sometimes you may need to be a bit flexible and accept a car to Bakersfield even if you want to end up in Los Angeles. The driver leaves a deposit, usually around $100, and picks it up from the company's office at the other end of the line once the car is safely delivered. The time and mileage allowed is limited, but it is sometimes possible to squeeze in a short excursion to a nearby sight. Such transport is available within the state of California as well, but cars between Los Angeles and San Francisco are not easily found and are snapped up quickly. Major cities in the country have such offices. Check in the phonebook under car transport, auto transport or drive-away.

## Roads

California has an excellent road system. Interstate and in-state freeways criss-cross the entire state. What they provide in directness, speed and convenience, however, is paid for by taking the boring route. Nothing can be more dangerously mesmerizing to a night driver than an endlessly flat and straight road with one white stripe after another passing in front of you. The driver who tries a backroad here and there and passes through tiny towns will enrich his or her visit.

Along the interstate highways, rest stops are interspersed. These usually include rest rooms, drinking water, a patch of green, some picnic tables, and perhaps a map and additional information about the area. It is perfectly okay to park here overnight and sleep in the car, and it's usually safe, especially if several large trailer trucks are parked nearby. People sometimes flop their sleeping bags down on the grass. Usually they are not disturbed, but officially it is not allowed.

## Some Driving Tips

In both San Francisco and Los Angeles, parking can be a problem. Parking is not allowed alongside red or white curbs, green curbs mean limited-time parking only and even at unpainted curbs parking may not be allowed during rush hours, street-cleaning hours, etc.

Right turns are allowed at red lights, unless otherwise indicated. Drive here as you would at a stop sign. At a marked crosswalk, drivers must yield to pedestrians. This can sometimes be annoying and some pedestrians exercise their power by giving a driver little time to stop. As a pedestrian, however, you will appreciate the law.

The maximum speed limit on highways and freeways is 55 miles per hour (88 kph), though there has been much grumbling about that, and on the L.A. freeways many drivers ignore the speed limit. In residential areas the speed limit is 25mph (40 kph). On main thoroughfares the speed limit may vary.

California has one of the strictest drunk-driving laws in the country, requiring the immediate arrest of anyone found to be driving under the influence of alcohol.

# INTRODUCTION

## Auto Clubs

The *American Automobile Association* is the best known of the auto clubs. Membership fees vary from state to state, ranging from about $20-$50. Services include trip planning, maps, travelers' checks (American Express) and — especially important — 24-hour emergency road service anywhere. Also worthwhile is the club's auto insurance.

In northern California, the AAA is listed as the California State Automobile Association. In southern California it is listed as the Automobile Club of Southern California (ACSC).

## Accidents

Call the police immediately in the event of any accident. On municipal streets, call the local police. On freeways, even within cities, and on highways and roads between cities, call the California Highway Patrol (CHP). On city freeways, the phones in the emergency callboxes link automatically to a CHP office. Otherwise, ask the operator for Zenith 1-2000, the CHP emergency number.

## Rides and Hitchhiking

Someone seeking a passenger to share expenses and company, or someone seeking a ride, would do well to check the nearest college or university. Most such centers have some sort of "ride board". Alternative radio stations and newspapers also provide this service.

Hitchhiking has declined a bit in California. A few gruesome incidents, with both drivers and passengers as the victims, have occurred, one's decision is a personal matter. Obviously, the vast majority of hitchhikers and helpful drivers are not hurt.

As either the driver or the rider, ask a few questions first before entering the situation, all the while trying to size up the person the best you can. In a region of a national park, a hitchhiker with a backpack standing in the middle of nowhere has probably just emerged from a trail and is trying to reach the nearest bank, shower and burger stand.

Hitchhiking within the city is generally less successful than between cities. It is generally easier to find the nearest bus.

Sometimes, if waiting by a restaurant or gas staion, approaching a driver will more likely get a positive response, but not always.

## Backpacking

California offers a whole world to explore for the packpacker. Information about backpacking is easily accessible, and trails in parks around the state are well-maintained.

# *I* NTRODUCTION

Numerous guide books on hiking and backpacking are available. Likewise, many stores sell camping equipment. Sometimes the big department stores and discount houses sell good equipment at cut-rate prices. Always check, though, that the equipment is of good quality.

Army-navy surplus stores, often found in the downtown sections of larger cities, can supply many of the smaller items. Today, camping has become a gigantic business, and new and improved equipment is produced anually. Everything but a jet-propelled backpack is on the market!

The *Sierra Club* is an excellent source of information for camping in California. Although a national conservation organization, the club originated in California. In addition to organizing hiking trips for members, the various branches will be able to provide printed guides and maps on specific regions in the state.

## Accommodations

The range of accommodation in California is almost unlimited. Luxurious hotels which look like old Roman villas, quaint lodges perched above the beach, sleazy downtown rattraps, sterile stucco motels, homey inns, and trailer campgrounds resembling suburbs on wheels — they are all here.

Lodging is not particularly cheap, and real bargains in overnight accommodation are hard to find. Most decent and reliable facilities, even in a standard motel, begin around $25.

Many local Chambers of Commerce distribute lists of local accommodation, as do visitors centers. Policies vary at these agencies about listing prices or making recommendations. Those who list accommodation are all members of the local chamber.

A list of suggested accommodation is available from the *California Hotel and Motel Association*, 414 29th st., Sacramento, CA 95816. Tel.916-444-5780.

Remember when considering price, that hotels in California tag on a hotel tax. This rate differs from area to area, ranging usually from 6% to as high as 10%.

The major hotel chains are well represented in both the major cities and outlying areas of California. In resorts, prices tend to rise on weekends. In major cities, hotels which cater to a business population and host conventions, often change things around: they offer discounts on weekends, which are sometimes very sizeable ones. This may be done on a haphazard basis by the individual hotel depending on the booking situation that weekend, or it may be part of a regular weekend special program followed in many branches of a hotel chain. This is worth checking out, for the reductions are substantial and allow for a luxurious weekend at very reasonable prices. Often these rates will only be mentioned upon request, so be sure to inquire about any weekend discount or special package. Below is a sampling of some of the available specials. The toll-free numbers listed are generally reservations and information numbers that give details about weekend specials or refer you to particular hotels. Even within a single hotel chain, the discount may vary from hotel to hotel, city to city or season to season.

*Best Western International*: tel. 800-528-1234. Discounts of 20-50% off regular rates.

*Hilton Hotels*: Various areas have their own 800 numbers. Ask specifically about the "Rainbow Weekend".

*Hyatt Hotels*: tel. 800-288-9000. Various weekend programs may include reductions of up to 50% on deluxe rooms.

*Marriott Hotels*: tel. 800-2888-9290. Ask about "Super Saver" and "Escape" packages for weekenders.

*Ramada Hotel Group*: tel. 800-272-6232. "R and R" weekend specials.

*Sheraton Hotels*: tel. 800-325-3535. Ask about "Time of your Life" weekends.

*Westin Hotels*: tel.800-228-300. Most have lower weekend rates.

*Motel 6* is a safe, standard, reliable and inexpensive motel-chain. Most have pools but television is extra. There is nothing surprising here, either pleasant or unpleasant. The price, about $21, is relatively inexpensive. There are about 400 motels in the chain nation-wide, and almost 100 in California alone. For a directory, write: *Motel 6*, Inc., 51 Hitchcock Way, Santa Barbara, CA 93105.

The Quest International hotel marketing organization, for a $99 annual membership fee, arranges a 50% discount off regular rates at more than 500 hotels in the United States, British Columbia and San Juan. The half-price reduction is offered no matter how seasonal prices may fluctuate. Quest International, Chinook Tower, Box 4041, Yakima, WA 98901, tel. 509-248-7512.

**Bed-Breakfast (B&B) Inns** have increased in number and popularity in recent years. There are several hundred scattered throughout California, but they are found predominantly in the north. They tend to be rustic and old. Some may be refurbished farmhouses, others old family-run hotels or Victorian houses. Each one is individual, expressing its own personality and that of its owners. Many are small, family-run operations, perhaps even in a wing of a private home. The rooms vary in style and furnishings and often there is an emphasis on old-time decor. Such inns may be located in the center of town, in completely residential areas, or in the country side. They can offer an inside glimpse of country life that hotel guests may not otherwise see. Staying at a B&B is a little more adventurous than staying in a conventional hotel. The atmosphere is often warm and casual, it is easy to meet the other guests or the owners. The breakfasts may include such touches as freshly-squeezed juice and home-baked muffins, as opposed to the standard coffee-shop fare. Often there are complimentary afternoon beverages, or use of the library or a bicycle, or other touches that make the experience more home-like.

There was a time when B&Bs were generally less expensive than hotels. Now the prices are on a par, and sometimes they are over-priced, not to mention outrageous. Nevertheless, there are plenty around which, while costing no more than the average motel, offer an individual experience to which a motel cannot compare. Because each inn is run at the fancy of its owner, features you would expect at a motel must be double-checked in a B&B: How big is the bed? Is the room furnished? Is the bathroom private? Is there a bath or only a shower? Are there any extras? Is breakfast full or continental (beverage, juice and rolls)? Are there weekday or off-season rates?

Various organizations who represent B&Bs in different regions have appeared, making it easier for the visitor to find a special one. These organizations know the characteristics of the different inns, and can also make suggestions and sometimes handle bookings.

Besides the B&Bs, there is also the "homestay", in which guests actually rent a room in a private residence. This can be less expensive and more homey than a B&B. Information is often available through the B&B associations.

In addition to the associations noted below, smalller organizations represent the inns of specific regions.

*Bed and Breakfast Innkeepers of Southern California*: P.O.Box 15385, Los Angeles 90015. tel. 805-966-0589.

*Bed and Breakfast Innkeepers of Northern California*: 2030 Union st., Suite 310, San Francisco 74123. tel. 415-563-4667.

*Association of Bed and Breakfast Innkeepers of San Francisco*: 737 Buena Vista W., San Francisco 94117. tel. 415-861-3008.

A brochure listing B&Bs throughout the state is published by the California Office of Tourism in Sacramento.

**Youth Hostels** provide another lodging alternative. A national network of Youth Hostels is operated by *American Youth Hostels* (AYH). The AYH is part of the *International Youth Hostel Federation*. Its membership card is valid for International Youth Hostel facilities. Conversely, a card from abroad is valid in the United States.

Hostel facilities are often found in schools, old hotels, and YMCAs, but sometimes they have their own buildings. Some hostels have smaller private rooms as well as dorm-like rooms, and most have kitchen facilities.

Youth hostels are by no means only for youth. Many others, such as professionals and seniors, use hostels in order to spice up their vacation. Hostels are ideal places for the lone traveler to strike up acquaintances and pick up travel tips.

Overnight fees are usually around $5-$6 for members, and a dollar or two more for non-members. AYH offices can be found in most major cities in the country.

In California there are over 30 hostels. Information can be obtained on them from your local AYH office. Some of the California hostels in which membership is sold include:

In San Francisco: 240 Fort Mason, S.F. 94123, tel. 415-771-7727.

In Los Angeles: 1502 Palos Verdes dr., N Harbor City 90710, tel. 213-831-8109.

In San Diego: Armed Services YMCA, 500 W. Broadway, SD 92101. tel. 619-232-1133.

The AYH operates other youth hostels as well in these metropolitan areas.

**YMCAs** have traditionally provided wayfarers with decent and simple lodgings, often in dormitories. Today they may range from the very inexpensive to the price of an average motel room. Usually, the price includes use of some or all of the sports facilities. The lodgings may range from shabby to sleek. Reservations are often recommended. For a listing of YMCAs and general information, contact: *The Y's Way*, 356 W. 34th st., New York, NY 10001. Tel. 212-760-5856. If you want a catalogue, send a self-addressed stamped envelope.

*The Young Women's Christian Association* (YWCA) offers the same type of lodging and facilities, but generally for women only. Contact: *The Young Women's Christian Association*, 726 Broadway, New York, N.Y. 10003. tel. 212-614-2700.

## Food

As with almost everything else in California, the world of food is rich, colorful and diverse. Eating out is a common pastime. Restaurants range from the elegant, elite and outrageously expensive to the incredibly cheap. In addition to American steak restaurants, Chinese and Mexican restaurants are extremely popular, widespread and accessible on any budget. More varieties of both Asian and Latin American food are becoming available. Italian restaurants are very common as well.

The grilling of fish and meats on mesquite coal is common in many California restaurants, especially in the north. There is an emphasis on fresh produce of excellent quality, mixed together in myriad ways. In recent years, with an increased emphasis on health, vegetarian cooking has developed into an art. Vegetarian restaurants are common, and serve a surprising variety of dishes, some tremendously imaginative. In conjunction with this is the increasingly common appearance of the salad bar, available as part of a larger meal or by itself. These salad bars are creations in themselves; the old days of tomatoes and shredded lettuce are gone. An average salad bar may include an array of cheeses and dressings, several kinds of nuts, potatoes, bread, fish, noodles and fruit — in other words, a salad can be a delicious and filling meal in itself. One of the best and most reliable salad bars can be found in the *Sizzler* chain of restaurants. The emphasis in this buffet type restaurant is on steak, but the salad bar, at about $4.25, is a welcome sight to those who prefer not to eat red meats.

Fast-food stands line the highways of California. They have branched out from the old simple burger stands and now include pizza, tacos, roast beef, chicken and ice cream. Prices at different branches of the same company are generally uniform. Occasionally, a chain will run some sort of special and proclaim it in the media, but sometimes a typical burger-fries-milkshake meal at a fast-food stand, besides containing dubious nutritional value, can cost as much as a sit-down meal at, for example, a small Chinese lunch counter.

The 24-hour coffee-shop chains form another characteristic California institution. They are far from the down-home diners of yesteryear. In each chain there are standardized designs, prices, menus, quality and employee uniforms. One can imagine that the same innocuous soft music plays simultaneously at hundreds of different coffee-shops.

However, there can be something comfortable about these places, especially when it is 2am and, up ahead at the next highway exit, the bright sign of a *Denny's*, *Sambo's*, *Norm's* or *Bob's* shines invitingly in the darkness. The soft lights, familiar booths, smiling waitresses, never-ending coffee and precisely sliced pie is somehow reliable and reassuring, even if rather bland.

Instead of tasting California's superb produce in a restaurant, it is possible to get it yourself direct from the farm. As mentioned throughout this book, many regions publish maps showing which local farms accept visitors, what the farm produces, etc. This is a good way not only to obtain fresh produce, but to break out of the tourist mold and meet the locals in an unusual setting. The produce you can sample ranges from vegetables and fruits to nuts, wines and cheeses. The regional directories can be obtained through local chamber of commerce offices, or through one central office: The Dept. of Food and Agriculture, 1220 N st., room 427, Sacramento 95814.

# *I*NTRODUCTION

## Parks and Reserves

### National Park Service (NPS)

An extraordinary diversity of preserved land is under the juristriction of the *National Park Service* including Yosemite, Death Valley, the Channel Islands and Redwood.

The park service enforces strict rules about the protection of natural areas. Entrance fees are charged and camping fees are extra, starting at $4. Fees for primitive campsites are nominal, and for backcountry free, but permits are required.

The *Golden Eagle Passport* allows unlimited entry into national parks for the holder and accompanying passengers in a single car. The pass costs $10 and can be purchased at a national park or NPS regional office.

The *Golden Age Passport* is free to seniors from age 62. It provides free life-time entry to all park lands, and 50% discounts on various fees, such as camping. Available at most national parks, it must be obtained in person. A similar pass, the *Golden Access Passport*, is available for blind and disabled individuals. This too must be obtained in person.

### National Forest Service

National Forest Service lands differ from National Parks in that they are multi-purpose. Logging and grazing, for example may be permitted under carefully controlled conditions. Few specific sites or regions are preserved for public visits, and there is not the same system of guided tours and activities as in National Parks. National forest land can, however, be stunning and certain areas have been designated as protected wilderness. There may be extensive trail networks throughout national forests. Camping is usually less expensive than in national or state parks, and in many areas it is free.

A new system allows campers to buy *camp stamps* at designated retail outlets or forest service offices, equal to the necessary camping fee. The user pays only 85% of the amount listed, thereby saving 15%. For further information contact *National Forest Service* headquarters in San Francisco.

### State Parks

California runs a huge state park system, with some land as stunningly beautiful as that protected in the state's national parks. There are extensive camping and hiking possibilities within the park system. With its mobile and recreation-oriented population, California's state parks can often be crowded. Campsites can cost $6 or more per vehicle, 50 cents for walk-ins and bicycles. Backcountry sites are generally free but permits may be required. At most parks reservations are accepted. They may be made through any *Ticketron* outlet (with an extra fee tagged on) or by a new reservation system called MISTIX. Call toll-free tel. 1-1800-I-GO-PARK.

## Practical tips for getting around

### Mail

Mail can be received at hotels. It can also be sent to the General Delivery of the post office of any city or town. In a large city, this is usually found in the main post office downtown. Users of *American Express* travelers' checks can use that company's offices to receive mail, but only if they previously request to do so.

#### Telephones

Telephone numbers are preceded by a 3-digit area code. There are 9 area codes within California. In some areas the boundary for area codes may fall within a populated area. Dialing from one area code to another, the prefix "1" must sometimes be added. By no means is it assured that within one area code all calls are local calls. In the Los Angeles area, with the recent splitting up of ATT, additional charges may be added to calls within the same area code. At public phones, local calls in some areas cost 20 cents. The phones take nickels (5 cents), dimes (10 cents), and quarters (25 cents). The operator is not needed to make a long-distance call from a pay phone. Just dial "1", the area code and the number, and an operator or a recording will tell you how much money is needed, so keep a pile of change handy. If an additional charge is owed at the end of the call, the phone will ring when you hang up.

Long-distance rates are substantially lower between 6pm and 8am, and on weekends from 11pm Friday to 5pm Sunday. For international calls, the lowest rates are between 3pm and 9pm.

Many companies now use toll-free numbers, recognizable by the 800 prefix to the number. No area code is necessary to call this number, but sometimes a "1" must precede the 800. An 800 number which is good for in-state calls may not be operable for calls from outside the state, and some companies have both in-state and out-of-state toll-free numbers. Local Yellow Pages list a company's toll-free numbers.

### Currency and Exchange

Foreign currency can be exchanged in international airports and certain banks. If possible buy travelers'checks in American dollars, at the appropriate exchange rate. Foreign currency will not be honored in the United States.

To send money to the United States it is best to give the name and address of an American bank correspondent to your bank at home. Money can be cabled, usually within 48 hours, for a charge of up to $25. A draft check, sent by mail, is a little cheaper but much slower.

## Banking

Banking hours in California are from Mon.-Thurs. 10am-3pm, and 10am-5pm on Fridays. Electronic tellers are now common and widespread among all major banks.

### Travelers' Checks

Travelers' checks are a must. They are available at banks or through organizations such as *American Automobile Association*, at a reduced price or at no charge.

*American Express* Travelers' Checks are the most widely recognized, and the company provides a measure of assistance and reassurance to those whose checks have been lost or stolen. *American Express Travel Service* offices will help arrange temporary identification, cash personal checks, arrange for new travelers' checks immediately, report and cancel credit card numbers and, in general, provide assistance. In addition, if arranged by mail beforehand, check holders may use the local *American Express* office as a mailing address.

### Credit Cards

A credit card is worth taking as an emergency source of cash or to pay for large items. Recognized credit cards will allow the holder to withdraw in cash the sum remaining in his credit. Make sure you know where to report a lost or stolen credit card, and do so immediately. Major credit cards such as *Visa*, *Mastercharge* and *American Express* are recognized throughout California. If coming from another country, check whether your credit card is affiliated with an American company. When using a credit card, always check the amount before signing, and be sure to get the receipt. In addition, ask for the black carbon and destroy it immediately. Occasionally, a business will want to keep the carbon. Refuse stubbornly and on all counts. Carbons have been used to produce counterfeit credit cards and should never leave the owner's possession. Likewise, never give your credit card number for identification purposes; use a passport or driver's license instead. Credit cards can also be used for long-distance calls in specially equipped public telephones.

# *I*NTRODUCTION

## Smoking, Alcohol, Drugs

Smoking is no longer "cool" in health-conscious California. It is prohibited by law in elevators, city buses and many public rooms, and is permitted only in restricted areas in restaurants and inter-city buses. Californians have become increasingly bold and insistent in requesting others in their proximity not to smoke.

The drinking age in California is 21. It is against the law to drive with an open container of alcohol in the car. Drunk-driving laws in California are strict and strictly enforced.

California is viewed by many as the land with a free-and-easy attitude towards drugs, especially marijuana. Possession of marijuana is no longer a felony, though one sometimes has to pay a fine. Marijuana is, frankly, very common and accepted, but it is not something to be brazen about and foreigners should be especially careful.

## Photography

If you are a photography buff, you will find ample material in California, among the stunning and diverse natural scenery and among the tremendous mixture of people and lifestyles.

If wanting to buy a camera, you might wait until you reach California, where competition is fierce, and many discount houses and department stores have camera departments which undercut the prices of regular camera shops. The camera shops, however, can give expert advice, which a clerk in a discount house is unlikely to have.

In the urban areas, one-hour and one-day developing services can easily be found. The large chain drugstores will often handle developing, and periodically run specials, such as two rolls for the price of one.

## Disabled Travelers

New hotels and other public buildings must, according to California law, be accessible by wheelchairs. Businesses and communities are becoming more aware of the needs of the disabled. Car rental companies can supply special cars for the disabled. *Greyhound, Trailways, Amtrak* and the airlines are now equipped to accommodate the disabled. Some companies give special rates to the disabled as well as to the elderly. Special parking spaces are reserved for the disabled.

For information on travel for the disabled, contact: The Society for the Advancement of Travel for the Handicapped, 26 Court st., Brooklyn, N.Y. 11242, tel. 212-858-5483.

## Senior Citizens

Many seniors are taking advantage of travel discounts and

programs oriented towards them. Discounts are available in theaters, museums, on public and private buses and in many other places. The American Association of Retired Persons (*AARP*) offers information on traveling for seniors, as well as considerable discounts on lodging and other travel expenses. For information, contact: AARP Membership Communications, 1909 K st. NW, Washington, DC 20049. tel. 202-872-4700.

## Important addresses and phone numbers

California is a very tourist-oriented state. Material written to assist vistors is voluminous and accessible, from public and commercial sources. The **California Office of Tourism** in Sacramento, will, for the price of postage, send its booklets to those interested. This office can provide a directory of Chambers of Commerce and Visitors' Bureaus throughout the state, a map and small pocket guide, a calendar of events, and a listing of Bed & Breakfast Inns. Write to: California Office of Tourism, Publications, 1121 L st., Suite 103, Sacramento, CA 95814. tel. 1-180-TO CALIF for toll-free information.

Some other useful addresses and numbers:
Department of Parks and Recreation: Distribution Center, P.O.Box 2390, Sacramento 95811. A guide to California's state parks is available for $2.00.
State Park Campground Reservations: tel. 1-1800-IGO-PARK.
National Park Service Information: 450 Golden Gate ave., San Francisco, CA 94102.
California Region, U.S. Forest Service: 630 Sansome st. San Francisco, CA 94111. For national forest information. A wide range of brochures available.
Ticketron Information: Northern California, tel. 414-393-4089 or 393-6914. Southern California, tel. 213-642-5870.
Department of Fish and Game: 1416 9th st. Sacramento, CA 95814. For fishing and hunting information and regulations.
U.S. Bureau of Land Management: 2800 Cottage Way, Sacramento, CA 95825. For a list of BLM campgrounds.
The Sierra Club: 530 Bush st., San Francisco, CA 94108. For information on California's ecological resources, as well as the clubs organized trips.
The Nature Conservancy: Western Regional Office, 425 Bush st., San Francisco CA 94108. Information on educational trips designed to teach about the environment.
The Wine Institute: 165 Post st., San Francisco, Ca 94108: A free booklet, *The Pleasure of Wine with Food* is available.
The local **Chamber of Commerce** of any city or small town is a resource worth exploring throughout your travels in California. These offices can tell you about small, obscure attractions that you might otherwise miss. The people in these offices are proud of their hometowns — sometimes inordinately so — and can share

unusual stories. In the popular resort areas, many Chambers of Commerce carry fliers with various discount coupons for sites in the area. Most interesting of all is the opportunity to meet people. If you express curiosity and interest in someone's hometown, you may be surprised at the open response.

## Electricity, Measurements, Time

**Electric current** is 110-115 a.c. 60Hz. For those planning to buy U.S. appliances, note that the U.S. plugs are two flat pins which will require adapters. Foreign appliances brought to the United States, generally require a transformer as well as an adapter.

**Measurements:** The U.S. measurement system is not a decimal one. Following are several conversion tables and "instant" tricks.

### Weight
28.349 grams — 1 ounce
0.453 kilograms — 1 pound

### Volume
0.473 liters — 1 pint
3.785 liters — 1 gallon

### Distance
2.540 cm — 1 inch
30.480 cm — 1 foot
0.914 meter — 1 yard
1.609 km — 1 mile

### Temperature
To convert Fahrenheit degrees to Centigrade (Celsius) subtract 32 from the Fahrenheit temperature, multiply by 5 and divide the total by 9.

### Time
All of California is within the Pacific Time Zone, which is GMT-8. This is one hour behind the Denver region, two hours behind Chicago and the Midwest, and three hours behind the East Coast. Daylight Saving Time begins on the last Sunday in April, and ends the last Saturday in October.

# CALIFORNIA

# CALIFORNIA

## San Diego

San Diego spreads around San Diego Bay on the California coast almost to the border of Mexico. Established in 1769 as a mission and presidio, it was the earliest settlement in California. In the not so distant past it had the image of a sleazy, run down sailors' town. Today, however, San Diego has been officially recognized as America's Finest City, something San Diegans were convinced of anyway. The physical setting is a stunning combination of ocean, mountain and desert. The cultural ambience is sophisticated and pleasure loving. There is always some festival being held under those endlessly bright skies, and there is a thriving theater scene and plenty of music from classical to jazz. Although it is California's second largest city with a population of about one million, in some ways San Diego has the atmosphere of a smaller city. Thus far it has managed to keep urban sprawl and congestion in check, and most of the main attractions are easily accessible by bus. There are many places just to stroll down and watch the passing crowd, and there are others where one can enjoy the sand and ocean undisturbed. Seventy miles (110 km) of beaches are punctuated by bluffs, coves and tidepools. The constant sea breezes keep the air fresh even in summer, and the winters are warm. People here love their outdoor recreation and there is plenty of it, from windsurfing to desert trekking. It is the kind of city which many flock to for a visit and end up staying.

Visitors can enjoy San Diego without a car. Many attractions appear in clusters: Point Loma, Balboa Park, Mission Bay, downtown and the waterfront, La Jolla and so forth. The bus system is extensive within the main urban radius. Within the main clusters of attractions, there is often plenty to explore on foot beyond the principal sites, even if only an old neighborhood or a stretch of beach and cliff. Bus routes extend everywhere within the main urban radius.

## How to get there

**By air:** The **San Diego International Airport** at Lindbergh Field straddles the northern curve of San Diego Bay. It is close to downtown, the resort hotels of Mission Bay, the string of motels north of Old Town, and the northern beaches. The airport has an east and a west terminal with information desks, transportation stations and **Traveler Aid** offices in each. Both public and private transportation are at hand. Unlike the Los Angeles Airport, the San Diego airport is not overwhelming.

**By land:** The main traffic artery reaching San Diego from the north is I-5, which runs parallel to and sometimes merges with the

# SAN DIEGO

*"Public transportation"*

Pacific Coast Highway. The drive between Los Angeles and San Diego takes about two hours along this freeway. I-5 runs into and through downtown and continues right to the border crossing with Mexico at San Ysidro. Coming from Los Angeles, the coastal route is more scenic, but slower. From Arizona, I-5 crosses the desert and the hothouse of the Imperial Valley toward the city.

**By Bus:** Downtown San-Diego is served by *Greyhound* (120 W. Broadway 239-9171) and *Trailways* (310 W.C. st. 232-2001). Many daily buses run to L.A. and another Californian locations.

**By train:** *Amtrak* station is on 1050 Kettner blvd. (tel. 800-USA-Rail) in downtown. Here you can take the *San Diegan* to L.A. and Santa-Barbara or the San Joaquin to San-Francisco.

## Public transportation

**Buses:** San Diego's *Metropolitan Transit System* (*MTS*) is a meshing of municipal, county and regional systems. All passes and transfers are reciprocal, and the systems interlock at various points. The nerve center of the system, and the place to go with any question or confusion, is the *Transit Store* at Broadway and 5th, downtown. Many bus lines converge in the immediate vicinity. The clerks there are helpful and patient, and any pass can be bought there. Ticket prices vary, depending on the system and distance. They start at 50 cents, with transfers starting at 25 cents. Exact change is required on buses. *Day Tripper* transit passes allow unlimited usage for one to three days for $3, $5 or $7. The *Regional Transit Guide*, available at the *Transit Store* or any public information office, details the extensive and sometimes complicated system. Please note that almost everyone drives a car in the city so the bus service is not very frequent and sometimes run an hour apart.

The *San Diego Trolley* leaves from 5:30am-9pm, from near the *Santa Fe Depot*, on C St. at Kettner, for the border crossing at San Ysidro. This is a good way to get to the Mexican border. The trolley is accessible by wheelchair.

You can travel virtually everywhere by bicycle in San Diego, from the northern coast to the Mexican border, and you need not be a champion racer. An extensive network of bicycle paths overlaps with a grid of specific bus routes for buses equipped with bicycle carriers. Using these bicycle carriers at no extra charge, a cyclist can catch a bus, hop off with his bicycle and ride to another point in the system where he can catch another bus. A detailed regional cycling map shows the cycling paths and the cycle-bus routes, stops, and parking lots with bike lockers. The map is free and is available from any Visitor Information Center and many bicycle stores. For information on bicycle routes, tel. 231-BIKE.

Public transportation is supplemented by a number of private companies operating buses and jitneys (passenger vans), many of which serve the military facilities, hotels and tourist attractions. Information for these can be found through a single clearinghouse, the *Commuter Computer*, tel. 237-POOL.

## Accommodations

Although San-Diego has many hotel and motel rooms you should reserve a room before arriving to the city in the tourist season. You can book a room by calling the hotel itself or by calling Toll-free 800-225-9610 outside California or 800-824-3051 in LA. This reservation service will find you a room according to your budget.

**Hotel Circle**, on both sides of I-8 just east of the junction with I-5, is just that: a circle with about as many standard hotels, motels, and coffee shops as you'll want to see at once. You can find just about anything you want here, from a **Motel 6** (tel. 296-1612) and several equivalents, to the expensive mini-kingdom of the *Town and Country Hotel*, (tel. 291-7131, 800-854-2608) where attendants on golf carts drive you to your room.

Groupings of resort hotels are found along the coast from Coronado in the south to La Jolla in the north, with many centered around Mission Bay and Mission Beach. The star of all these is the *Hotel del Coronado*, dating from 1887. Two man-made islands, Shelter Island and Harbor Island, offer boating and marina activities, and both have stylish restaurants and hotels. Harbor Island is just south of the airport.

The downtown area has some old residential hotels as well as newly refurbished luxury hotels such as the *U.S. Grant.* Some of the old residentials may seem like bargains, but location is crucial; be wary of anything too far south of Broadway.

The neighborhood around the train station is better. East of downtown, on El Cajon blvd., toward San Diego State University, there are many inexpensive motels.

San Diego has some bed and breakfast inns, but not in the same profusion as smaller cities up north. A referral service can help you find one: *San Diego Bed & Breakfast Register*, P.O. Box 22948. San Diego 92122, tel. 560-7322 or 453-6745.

## Very expensive

*Hotel del Coronado:* 1500 Orange ave., Coronado 92118, tel. 435-6111. The king of hotels, the hotel of kings. Its restaurants are ranked among the best in San Diego. $120 up.

*U.S. Grant Hotel:* Downtown, 326 Broadway, tel. 232-3121. Very elegant hotel from 1910. Renovated and reopened some years ago.

## Expensive

*Britt House:* near Balboa Park, 460 Maple st., tel. 234-2926. Only 10 rooms in a charming Victorian inn. Bath for every two rooms.

*Dubletree Hotel:* Hotel Circle, 901 Camino del Rio, tel. 543-9000. Modern and comfortable. Special floors for nonsmokers.

*Colonial Inn:* La Jolla, 910 Prospect st., tel. 454-2181, 800-832-5525. A very good place to stay in the heart of La Jolla. Victorian style architecture and charming elevator.

## Moderate

*Torrey Pines Inn:* 11480 Torrey Pines rd., tel. 453-4420. A little bit out of town (between Del Mar and La Jolla) but very quiet and a wonderful view of the Pacific coast.

*Hotel Churchill:* (B&B) 827 C st., 92101, tel. 234-5186. In-state toll-free, tel. 800-621-5650, then 168-802. About 100 rooms, centrally situated in downtown. A variety of rooms. $40 and up.

*Hanalei Hotel:* 2770 Hotel Circle N., tel. 297-1101. In-state toll-free Tel. 800-542-6082; out-of-state toll-free, tel. 1-800-854-2608. Stylish, with a conspicuous Hawaiian motif. Very popular. $65 up.

## Inexpensive

*Western Shores Motel:* 4345 Mission Bay dr., 92109. tel. 273-1121. Across from Mission Bay golf course, near Sea World. Short walk to the bay. $29 up.

*Old Town Budget Inn:* Old Town, 4444 Pacific hwy, tel. 260-8024. Good rates for a clean and simple motel. Helpful management.

*E-2 8 Motels:* very simple but the most inexpensive motel chain in town. 4 locations: Hotel Circle (tel. 291-8252), Old town (tel. 294-2512), Mission Valley (tel. 223-9500), Downtown (tel. 462-7022). Call for reservations.

There are four American Youth Hostels in the area: *Imperial Beach* (tel. 423-8039), *Point Loma* (tel. 223-4778) and two in San Diego. For more information call the main facility, 1031 India st. (tel. 239-2644).

**Camping**: There is no camping in the city itself. Near State Beach camping facilities are found in South Carlsbad, San Elijo, and Silver Strand south of Coronado. tel. 237-6770. Camping reservations are made through Tel. 1-800-446-PARK. Koa site located in Chulavista about 10 miles (16 km) south of San-Diego (tel. 427-3601).

The County Dept. of Parks and Recreation has its own system of campgrounds, many in the mountain and desert areas, tel. 565-3600. For camping within the Cleveland National Forest, call headquarters at tel. 293-5050.

## Food

There is no shortage of restaurants here, and there is a proliferation of fast-food stands as well. There are clusters of elegant restaurants, at Shelter Island, Mission Bay and Coronado.

There are many elegant restaurants around the resort areas in San Diego, but the city is best known for its outstanding Mexican food. It abounds with excellent Mexican restaurants, some are lavishly ornamented with *pinata* and other south-of-the-border kitsch, while others are tiny downtown storefronts with formica counters, a table or two, and mouth-sizzling, filling portions.

Many elegant restaurants are concentrated in the main resort areas: Mission Beach, Mission Bay, La Jolla, Coronado, and the Gaslamp Quarter. The Embarcadero has a wide range of seafood restaurants. The restaurants in La Jolla tend to be expensive, but there are some surprises.

*Chuey's Cafe*: 1894 Main st., Barrio Logan. A local favorite. Don't be put off by the Quonset hut. Huge portions, excellent food and reasonable prices.

*Casa de Bandini*: 2654 Calhoun st., in Old Town. Festive feeling amid fountains. Fantastic food.

*Anthony's Seafood Mart*: 555 Harbor Lane. Quick service, fresh seafood, filling and fair.

*New Peking*: 807 Broadway, downtown. A great Chinese buffet, all you can eat. A good bargain.

*Garcia's of Scottsdale*: 3106 Sports Arena blvd. in Point Loma area, in Glasshouse Square. A bright Mexican setting, interesting combinations for those unfamiliar with the food. Heavy on the guacamole and sour cream.

# DOWNTOWN SAN DIEGO

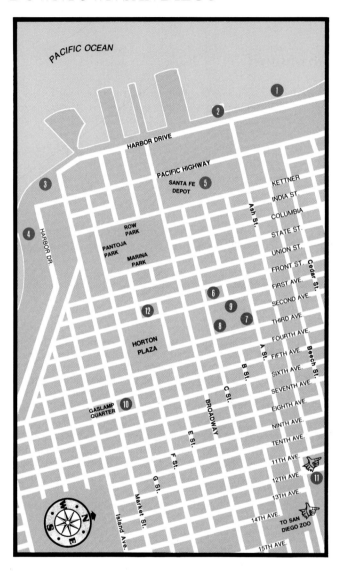

PACIFIC OCEAN

HARBOR DRIVE

PACIFIC HIGHWAY

SANTA FE DEPOT

KETTNER
INDIA ST.
COLUMBIA
STATE ST.
UNION ST.
FRONT ST.
FIRST AVE.
SECOND AVE.
THIRD AVE.
FOURTH AVE.
FIFTH AVE.
SIXTH AVE.
SEVENTH AVE.
EIGHTH AVE.
NINTH AVE.
TENTH AVE.
11TH AVE.
12TH AVE.
13TH AVE.
14TH AVE.
15TH AVE.

Ash St.
Cedar St.
Beech St.

ROW PARK
PANTOJA PARK
MARINA PARK

HORTON PLAZA

GASLAMP QUARTER

HARBOR DR.

A St.
B St.
C St.
BROADWAY
E St.
F St.
G St.
Market St.
Island Ave.

TO SAN DIEGO ZOO

**Index**

1. Embarcadero
2. Maritime Museum
3. Harbor Seafood Mart
4. Seaport Village
5. Santa Fe Depot
   Information Center
6. Chamber of Commerce
7. Convention and Visitors Bureau
8. Civic Theater
9. Convention and Performing Arts Center
10. Gaslamp Quarter
11. Balboa Park
12. International Visitor Information Center

## Downtown

Financier Alonzo Horton was convinced, in the 1860s, that San Diego would burgeon if located closer to the port. He bought a tract of neglected land at about 27 cents per acre and distributed it — gratis — to parties who promised to build there. Thus, "New Town" was born and "Old Town" was doomed. The appearance changed with the location, and adobe was replaced by the Victorian style.

Downtown centered around 5th Avenue and from there spread north, but the district, which became known as the **Gaslamp Quarter,** fell into disrepute, and became a haven for prostitutes, criminals and rowdy visiting sailors. By the 1900s the original core of downtown was deserted; the quarter continued to decay and never recovered.

In recent years civic groups have worked to restore the Gaslamp Quarter. They received a boost when the neighborhood was declared a Nationally Registered Historic District. Currently it is still part antique store and polished bar, part pornotheater and fleatrap hotel.

Between 4th and 6th aves., and L st. and Broadway, the Gaslamp area invites daytime browsing and exploration. The buildings are being refurbished with great care, their exquisite details honed and polished. Stylish restaurants, wood paneled and filled with ferns, are springing up and some of the tiny storefront diners still serve great meals. Today, murals add to the atmosphere of the quarter. One of the largest, on the south wall of the **Gollan Hotel** at 5th and Island, depicts a turn of the century scene, but with the faces of today's Gaslamp characters.

The intimate **Gaslamp Quarter Theater**, 547 4th ave., tel. 234-9583, is housed in an old 1920s dance hall and stages professional productions. Note the box office, which is the original dance hall ticket booth. The *Gaslamp Quarter Foundation*, in the **William Heath Davis House**, 410 Islan ave. ($2 donation per person is requested) tel. 233-4694, conducts tours of the quarter on Saturday at 10am and 1pm.

Just west of the Gaslamp Quarter, along Broadway, is **Horton Plaza,** the bright and crowded shopping hub of a revitalized downtown. The multi-storied complex, part of which resembles a multi-colored battleship prow, features street performers and live music during the day. The **International Visitor Information Center** is located under the shopping level of the plaza, with its entrance at 1st ave. and F st., tel. 236-1212.

## The Embarcadero

Once teeming with steamers and sailing ships, San Diego's harbor today is dominated by fishing fleets (tuna is the main catch), pleasure crafts and naval vessels. The city is essentially a massive naval base with approximately 100,000 active sailors and marines on any given day. The **Embarcadero** area, a popular spot with visitors, is concentrated between **Seaport Village Shopping Center** in the south and the **Maritime Museum** in the north. The walk is easy and refreshing, offering peaceful views across the bay, with a gleaming skyline. If you enjoy seafood, visit the **Harbor Seafood Mart** with its fresh fish markets and restaurants. Just north of the mart, at the **G Street Mole**, many of the large tuna seiners pull in. Look at the immense piled up nets. The cruise ships dock at the **Broadway Pier** and **B Street Pier** to allow passengers to board or disembark. Several companies offer excursions around the bay.

Nearby, at the Embarcadero and Harbor drive is the **San Diego Maritime Museum**. Open daily, 9am-8pm. Adults $4; seniors, military and age 13-17, $3, tel. 234-9153. The museum is comprised of three ships: an old San Francisco ferry, an old luxury yacht and a 19th century square-rigged cargo vessel, the **Star of India**. This is the centerpiece of the museum. The oldest merchantman afloat, this ship circled the globe many times, carrying emigrants from England to Australia, and bearing cargoes of timber and salmon.

# Balboa Park

Balboa Park extends almost as far as downtown, yet it has a sheltered and other-worldly atmosphere. The Spanish buildings are graceful and exquisite, the gardens blazing with color. It is a pleasure to wander along the quiet paths among the art studios in the re-created Spanish village. There are also a number of museums here, and the world-famous San Diego Zoo.

The Spanish buildings were built for the 1915 Panama-California Exposition, which marked the completion of the Panama Canal. San Diego was to be the first American port reached by ships cutting westward through the canal, and the city went all out for the celebration. A whole Spanish mini-city was created, and the buildings standing today are but a small remainder of those built for the celebrations.

The main concourse is **El Prado**, leading from Laurel st. to the **Plaza de Panama**. This plaza is the center of the park. Just east of the plaza is the **House of Hospitality**. The information center here, 1549 El Prado, open 9:30am-4pm daily, tel. 239-9628, can supply brochures and details on museums and activities in the park, as well as general city-wide information. Be sure to ask about any upcoming concerts or performances because there is always something going on in the park. Glance into the central courtyard at the sculpture of an Aztec woman pouring water.

The array of museums concentrated in this park is mind-boggling.

*Horton Plaza — multi-storied and multi-colored complex*

One could easily spend a few days here doing nothing but museum-hopping. On the first Tuesday of every month entry to the museums is free.

The **Botanical Building** offers guided tours of its tropical and semi-tropical plants. At the **Spreckels Organ Pavillion**, the largest outdoor organ in the world is played during free recitals every Sunday at 2pm. The **Museum of Art** displays masterpieces which include examples of modern American realism, in addition to the works of Henry Moore and Alexander Calder. You can also enjoy a cup of coffee in the **Sculpture Garden Cafe**. The sculptures on the entrance facade are of 17th-century Spanish painters, including El Greco. The adjacent **Timkin Art Gallery** displays work by El Greco, as well as by Rembrandt, Brueghel and others.

In the planetarium of the **Reuben H. Fleet Space Theater and Science Center** the sophisticated equipment makes you feel as if you have been seized and hurled into the galaxy. The range of shows is expansive, including music from the rock group Pink Floyd, and a stunning visual trek into the Grand Canyon. There are children's workshops, free films and ongoing, ever-changing demonstrations. Other interesting places to visit include the **Centro Cultural de la Raza**, with its exciting Chicano murals, and the **Museum of Photographic Arts**, in the Casa De Balboa on the Prado. This museum is a gem. Exhibits have included the black-and-white works of virtuosos such as Ansel Adams and Henri Cartier-Bresson, as well as bright and abstract experiments in

*Strolling around Seaport Village*

all sorts of photographic media. The bookstore located here also makes for interesting browsing.

Other museums include the **Museum of Man**, the **Aero-Space Museum** at the end of the Pan American Plaza, the **Museum of San Diego History**, the **Model Railroad Museum** and the **Hall of Champions** honoring San Diego's star athletes. The **Natural History Museum** presents the regional wildlife found in the diverse surrounding ecological regions. It also sponsors whale watching trips in the winter, though places must be reserved in advance. The **Old Globe Theater**, near the Plaza de Panama, resembles the original theater in London. Here, and at the adjacent **Cassius Carter Center Stage**, Shakespearean and other productions are staged. Tours of the theaters and backstage area are given on weekends at 11am.

Just north of the Natural History Museum, the small neat cottages of the **Spanish Village** house studios for potters, woodworkers, weavers and other craftsmen. The quality here is generally very high. Visitors are free to observe, browse and buy.

Just a bit further along is the 1910 **carousel**, where you can ride on a hand-carved giraffe, dragon, ostrich or zebra. Pull the brass ring, win a free ride and impress your companion. At 50 cents per ride, it's a bargain.

A visit to the justly famous **San Diego Zoo** deserves a full day. Admission $8.50, under 16 $3.50, under 3 free. Deluxe tours are available. On Founder's Day in early October, admission is free. Open July through Labor Day, 9am-5pm; Post-Labor Day through June 9, 9am-4pm, tel. 234-3153 or 231-1515.

The hundred acres of exotic gardens and superb recreations of the animals' natural habitats are marvelous. Some of the world's rarest animals are found here. Because of the mild, steady climate there is no need for closed shelters.

The zoo is as concerned with preserving and breeding rare species as it is with showing them to the public. The Galapagos Turtle and Koala Bear are among the endangered species which find sanctuary here. The zoo offers some bus tours and sky rides which are better to avoid. The zoo shop near the entrance is the right place to buy some of the best T-shirts in the country.

## Old Town

**Old Town San Diego State Historical Park**, wedged between I-8 and I-5, is a combination of historical sites and tourist shops. Explor among the adobe brick buildings, with their rough hewn doors and beams, and sense the atmosphere of the original village that sprang up here to become the city of San Diego. More information can be obtained at the **Visitor and Information Center**, 2645 San Diego ave., tel. 237-6770.

Gaspar de Portola, a Spanish commander, and Padre Junipera Serra initiated settlement in San Diego and California in 1769, with the establishment of the presidio and a mission on the adjacent hill. The mission later moved but the presidio remained. As retired soldiers and other settlers sought homes, the small village spread below the presidio, in a typical settlement pattern. Its growth continued after Mexico won independence and stripped the mission of its lands. Americans also arrived here, some as sailors on the Yankee merchantmen that shipped tallow and hides to the eastern seaports. When the U.S. took over San Diego after the Mexican War, American settlement naturally increased, and the town took on a more American character. Some of the settlers had witnessed all three periods of rule, as did the village itself, with its smattering of stately Spanish baronial, plebian pueblo brick, and clapboard-and-frame architecture.

In 1867 the town's fortunes plunged when financier Alonzo Horton initiated the building of a new town. The old town declined and a fire then destroyed most of it. It remained a ruin until historical renovation began.

Most of the remaining Old Town structures are included within the state park. The Park Service conducts a free one-hour walking tour everyday which leaves at 2pm from the **Casa de Machado-Silvas**, near the plaza. The park information center, at the corner of San Diego and Mason, provides information for self-guided tours. The **Casa de Machado-Stewart**, mentioned in Richard Henry Dana's *Two Years Before the Mast*, suggests the simple and hardy life of an early settler. The **Casa de Bandini** emanates old-world elegance (and houses an excellent restaurant), as does the **Casa de Estudillo**, where Don Jose Antonio Estudillo managed to maintain his public positions through three separate national reigns. In 1867 two partners launched a newspaper in a small general store on Twiggs St., and today that newspaper, the *San Diego Union*, has bought its birthplace and turned it into a small newspaper museum.

The **Historical Museum** displays a model of Old Town in 1870. A collection of horse-drawn vehicles fills Seeley Stables. The old schoolhouse is worth visiting at as well.

The Presidio is a gentle uphill walk from Old Town — there's no need to get in your car again. The **Serra Museum** sits on the site of the original mission within the bounds of the old presidio. A replica of the original mission, the museum is the headquarters for the *San Diego Historical Society* and features exhibits from the Indian, Spanish and Mexican periods.

# Coronado

It is a beautiful drive from downtown San Diego to the peninsula of Coronado, along the **Coronado Bridge** which curves across the bay like a ribbon lifted by the breeze. The centerpiece of Coronado, which is a small separate community once reached only by ferry or a long southern detour, is the **Hotel del Coronado**. Built in 1887 as a seaside resort, this multi-turreted and gilded masterpiece has hosted royalty, dignitaries and American presidents from Benjamin Harrison to Ronald Reagan. The hotel has also been used as a location for filming. The lobby and main dining room are dazzling. Feel free to wander, especially in the Hall of History, where old newspaper clippings tell the story of a bygone age.

In the neighborhood there are several stately turn-of-the-century mansions. **Silver Strand State Park**, south of Coronado, has some nice beaches on the bayside. The Coronado Municipal Beach, comprising virtually the whole shore, is a popular swimming beach.

# Point Loma

At the tip of Point Loma, the **Cabrillo National Monument** juts south into the Pacific. Juan Rodriguez Cabrillo was the first to discover and enter San Diego Bay, which he described as a harbor "closed and very good". The natives who greeted the ships, he remarked, were "comely and large".

In the visitor center there are exhibits on Cabrillo and the main features of the park; the Bayside Trail winding down to the eastern shore; the tidepools pounded by Pacific surf along the western shore, the 1859 lighthouse and the whale overlook. The visitor center presents a regular schedule of programs guided by rangers. Open daily 9am-5:15pm, tel. 557-5450.

The monument is a prime spot to observe the annual southern migration of the Gray Whales, which occurs between late December and the end of February. The whales pass Point Loma on their way from the Arctic Ocean to the lagoons of Baja California, where the pregnant females bear their calves. From the overlook the whales are visible beyond the kelp beds. During the migrations rangers present programs on the natural history of the whales.

The rhythms of marine life can be more closely observed among the rocky tidepools on the monument's Pacific shore. Best visited during the low tides of autumn, winter and spring, the pools allow glimpses of anemones, limpets, starfish, crabs and an occasional octopus.

On the western edge of Point Loma, north of the national monument, begin the beautifully sculpted **Sunset Cliffs**, paralleled by Sunset Cliffs Boulevard. The shoreline here is rippled with tidepools, and is particularly beautiful at sunset.

**Ocean Beach**, further north, is a favorite teenage hangout and surfing beach where surfboards can be rented. The municipal pier is well-known for its fishing, and surf boards can be rented here too. During the day, it seems that all the radios on the beach are tuned in to the same punk station, and at night the dark beach glitters with bonfires. Newport ave., the main drag for a few blocks, has some "down-home" restaurants which serve generous and reasonably priced breakfast and lunch specials. Lodging on Newport is sparse and not especially appealing.

## Mission Bay

Mission Bay Park, a small resort just north of the airport, is a maze of waterways and islands. Its attractions include shoreline walks, swimming, sports, fishing, boating and cycling. Some luxury hotels perch over the water. Just off I-5, along the eastern edge of Mission Bay, is a visitor information center, which is clearly marked from the highway, 2688 E. Mission Bay dr., tel. 276-8200.

Along the narrow peninsula, extending north from the bay, one can take a walk either along the bay side or the ocean side. Try to plan it for sunset. A stern-wheeler plies the waters between the *Bahia Hotel*, near the southern end of this strip, and the *Catamaran Hotel* at the northern end.

**Sea World** is the star attraction of Mission Bay and one of the most

*Mission Bay*

famous tourist attractions nation-wide. Baby Shamu the whale is the starsof Sea World. Open 9am-dusk daily, summer season until 10pm. Adults $20; seniors and ages 3-11, $17.75. Special fares after 5pm, special facilities for the handicapped, tel. 226-3901; or in Los Angeles, tel. 714-826-7213. In addition to the elaborate animal shows, there are collections of animals including sharks and a colony of penguins in a simulated arctic environment. The coral reefs and the fish swimming among them are dazzling. Hydrofoil and other rides are available. Various touring companies serve Sea World, as do public buses. If you are arriving by car, take the exit west from I-5 on Sea World Drive.

On the ocean side of Mission Bay, **Mission Beach** and **Pacific Beach** are two more links in the chain of beautiful swimming beaches. **Ocean Front Walk** is a popular stretch for jogging and cycling.

## La Jolla

Academia and entrenched wealth form a strange blend in La Jolla, a beautiful semi-separate community perched on its own small promontory and beach, north of the city center. The **University of California at San Diego (UCSD)** is located here. The town is famous for its small sea cave and the adjacent cove which is a favorite scuba diving spot. **Windansea** and **Tourmaline** are both popular surfing and swimming beaches. Expensive boutiques, galleries and restaurants line **Prospect Avenue** above the beaches.

The **La Jolla Museum of Contemporary Art**, is devoted to the trends of minimal, pop, abstract, modern and post-modern art at 700 Prospect st. Open Tues., Thurs. and Fri. 10am-5pm; Wed. 10am-9pm; Sat. and Sun. 12:30-5pm. Admission charge, tel. 454-3541. The **Mingei International Museum of World Folk Art** has an eclectic collection of folk arts and crafts as well as programs in folk music. Don't let the setting, a shopping mall, thwart you, 4405 La Jolla Village dr. Open Tues.-Sat., 11am-5pm, Sun., 2-5pm. Donations suggested, tel. 453-5300.

North of the bluffs, along North Torrey Pines rd., is the **Torrey Pines Glider Port**, where hang-gliders gracefully leap into nothingness. The less adventurous can take some great photos here.

UCSD consists of four separate colleges on one campus, each college with its own theme and architecture. Attached to the University is the famous **Scripps Institution of Oceanography**, one of the finest oceanographic research centers in the world, Its aquarium and museum present a fascinating insight into the marine world, through such devices as its tidepool models. 8602 La Jolla Shores dr. Open daily 9am-5pm. Admission free, tel. 452-6933.

On North Torrey Pines rd., the strange jutting corners of concrete belong to the **Salk Institute for Biological Studies**. Tours offered from Mon.-Fri. 10:30am-3pm. Though research in many fields is conducted here, there is great focus upon neurological functions.

North of La Jolla, on North Torrey Pines Rd., extending almost to Del Mar, is the **Torrey Pines State Reserve**. Only one other grove of such trees exists, on the Channel Island. The scraggly trees grow in strangely sculpted beds of eroded sandstone. It is pleasant hiking among the trees and along the beach, tel. 755-2063.

## Important addresses and phone numbers

San Diego Convention and Visitor Bureau: 1200 3rd ave., suite 824, tel. 232-3101 or tel. 239-9696 (tape-recording of events).
Visitors Information Center: 2688 E. Mission Bay dr., tel. 276-8200.
International Visitor Information Center: 1st ave. & F st. (in Horton Plaza), tel. 236-1212.
San Diego Council American Youth Hostels: 1031 India st., tel. 239-2644. Will supply list of hostels in other areas.
Travelers Aid: Airport, tel. 231-7361.
Travelers Aid: 1122 4th ave, suite 201, tel. 232-7991. 24 hr. service.
Tijuana Tourism and Convention Bureau: 7860 Mission Center Court, Suite 202, 92108, San Diego, tel. 298-4105.
National Park Information: tel. 237-6770.
Public Transit Information: tel. 233-3004. 5:30am-8:25pm.
Commuter Computer: tel. 237-POOL.
Bicycling Information: tel. 231-BIKE.
Beach and Surf Conditions: tel. 225-9492.
Weather: tel. 289-1212.
Arts/Entertainment Hotline: tel. 234-ARTS.
Area Code: 619.

# Around San Diego

From the area north of the San Diego urban area, to Orange County and the lower reaches of the Los Angeles urban octopus, the coastal highway is studded with small beach towns. A string of state beaches and state parks line the shoreline, some with camping facilities. The mountains recede inland from the beach.

Northeast of San Diego, near Escondido and still in San Diego County, is the **Wild Animal Park**, run under the same auspices as the celebrated San Diego Zoo. Open daily from 9am-dusk and until 8pm in summer weekends. Ticket package, including monorail and all amenities, is half the price of the San Diego Zoo. Admission without monorail available, tel. 619-234-6541. Here, however, it is

*Wild animals at the Wild Animal Park*

the visitor who is enclosed while traversing the animals's turf. The monorail carries you along the five-mile tour through this 1,800 acre reserve, where herds of animals from Africa, Asia and Australia graze. During the summer there are evening trips as well. If you wish to visit just one zoo in the area, it is a good idea to come here instead of the famous San-Diego Zoo.

The Animal Park can be reached from San Diego by following the I-15 north, to **Via Rancho Parkway**, and then following the signs. Public transportation is available from **Escondido**. *Gray Line* offers tours from San Diego which include admission and monorail.

Two other attractions in the San Diego area are the Bird Sanctuary in Chulavista and the Julian Gold-Town. The **Nature Interpretive Center** located in 1000 Gunpowder Point Dr. From San Diego take interstate 5 to E St. exit in Chulavista or take the San-Diego trolley the Bay Front/E St. station. In the nature center you can see different fishes and reptiles, but the most interesting are the birds. Some 130 species of them live freely here (open Tues.-Sun. 10am-5pm. Admission free. Tel. 619-422-BIRD).

**Julian** was once a gold winning town during the gold rush era, more than a hundred years ago. Today you can still enjoy the old west feeling in a genuine atmosphere rather than a tourist trap. Today you can visit the beautiful 100 years old **Julian Hotel** (Main and C. St.), The **Julian Pioneer Museum** (Washington and 4th St., tel. 765-0227) or enjoy apple pie, the delicatessen of the area, in the famous **Julian Cafe** (2112 Main St., tel. 765-2712). If you are fed up with plastic San-Diego and the highway asphalt scenery, this is the place to go. If you wish to stay overnight, you may try the expensive Julian Hotel (tel. 765-1420) or settle for the **YMCA** at **Camp Marston** (tel. 765-0692) west of town. The best way to get to Julian is by taking Hwy 78 east of I 15 or by the *Northeast Rural Bus System* (tel. 619-765-1857).

**Oceanside** is an ordinary beach town, a watering hole for the Marines stationed at adjacent Camp Pendleton. Route 76, heading northeast from town into the mountains, climbs into some beautiful, rugged country and passes some interesting sites. Five miles up the road, **Mission San Luis Rey** overlooks a lovely valley. Founded in 1789, this was at one time the largest and most populous Indian mission in both Americas. In mid-July stop in for the fiesta. (Open daily, tel. 619-757-3651.)

Further up on Route 76 is the **San Antonio de Pala Mission**, a branch of the mission down below. Open daily 10am-15pm except Monday. The rough-hewn building with the Indian paintings gives one a better impression of what life must have been like here than the slicker renovations in other missions. There is a cemetery with hundreds of unmarked Indian graves.

The road dips into the Pauma Valley and winds upward toward the silver dome of the **Palomar Observatory**. Open daily 9am-4pm, tel. 619-742-3476. Operated by the **California Institute of Technology**, it holds some of the biggest and most advanced telescopes in the world. The tour includes a museum and exhibit hall presenting celestial photographs. It is advisable to bring a sweater as the dome can be chilly.

The **Palomar Mountain State Park** and the adjoining **Cleveland National Forest** contain low canyons and high peaks, pine forests, and several short nature trails. Camping facilities are available. Headquarters are in Escondido, tel. 765-0755.

# Toward Mexico

South of the town, **San Ysidro** is the entrance to Mexico, an arch extending over 16 lanes of traffic. Two miles beyond that is the city of Tijuana.

## Tijuana

Tijuana is a major international tourist attraction. Traffic floods over the border into the teeming city center. It was once a rather sleazy tourist trap, but now is much more attractive, and even if it is not absolutely authentic, it is bustling and exciting and very different from its northern neighbor San Diego.

The main street, **Avenida Revolucion**, is for seven blocks a lively gallery of tacky, cheap and gawdy displays. The **Tijuana Tourist Information Booth** is at 4th and Revolucion. At 8th and Revolucion you can see the ornate and gracious **Fronton Palacio**, a city landmark and the home of the fast-moving *Jai alai* games, held Fri.-Wed., throughout the year, with *pari-mutuel* betting. On some of the side streets, and on **Constitucion**, which parallels the main street, the shops are smaller and geared more to locals than tourists.

If you search through the trinkets, some good handicrafts can be found: bright tiles, hand-tooled leather, pottery etc. With the city's status as a free port, foreign imports such as French perfumes and Belgian glass can be more easily acquired.

Tijuana has two bullrings. **El Toreo**, just south of downtown, presents fights each Sunday from spring through fall. **Plaza Monumental**, five miles west of downtown toward the ocean, is second in size only to the one in Mexico City. Thoroughbred and greyhound racing at the **Hippodrome**, south of El Toreo, is also a major attraction.

**Ensenada** is famous for its sports fishing. It is about 70 miles south of Tijuana on the Baja Peninsula in a protected harbor, and is accessible from Route 1. Try the lobster restaurants along the road. The pace is relaxed and quiet compared to Tijuana. **Punta Banda**, at the tip of the bay's southern promontory, is famous for its sea geyser, shooting up as the powerful surf crushes against the coast.

East of Tijuana, along Mexican Route 2 is **Mexicali**, the capital of Baja, and comparable in size to Tijuana. It can also be reached by Route 80 on the California side, as the highway passes through Calexico. Devoid of Tijuana's colorful hustle, it still has many restaurants, shops and local entertainment spots.

## How to get there

San Diego Metropolitan Transit buses and a light rail trolley head for the border, and from there cabs are available to Tijuana, for about $1. The trolley leaves from the Amtrak depot at **Santa Fe Station**. *Mexicoach* and *Greyhound* have daily service to Tijuana. In addition, *Grayline* operate tours.

### Border Formalities

Holders of U.S. citizenship do not require a visa for travel to Mexico. If you travel more than 75 miles, or stay in Mexico more than 72 hours, a tourist card is required. This is obtainable free from the Mexican Consulate or *Mexican Government Tourist Office*, for those with proper U.S. identification. Citizens of other countries will also require tourist cards, and sometimes also a visa. They should inquire at the Mexican Consulate. To re-enter the United States, foreign citizens must have valid multiple entry visas and passports, except Canadians, who need only show proof of Canadian citizenship.

**Auto insurance**
If driving in Mexico, auto insurance is essential; an accident can be a criminal offence. Insurance for Mexico must be handled by a Mexican agency. No American or foreign agent is licensed to sell auto insurance for Mexico. A number of Mexican firms have offices in San Diego. Some can be found on the road to San Ysidro. The *Convention and Visitors' Bureau* in San Diego can also suggest firms.

## Important addresses and phone numbers

Mexican Consulate: 225 Broadway, Suite 225, San Diego 92101. Tel. 619-231-8414, or 125 Paseo de la Plaza, Los Angeles 90012. Tel. 213-624-3261.

Mexican Tourist Office: 600 B St., Suite 1220 San Diego 92101. Tel. 619-236-9314, or 9701 Wilshire Blvd., Beverly Hills 90212. Tel. 213-274-6315.

# The California Desert

Hemming in the packed urban areas of Los Angeles and San Diego from the east are several mountain ranges, beyond them lies the California desert. The desert actually comprises the bulk of what we generally refer to as Southern California. The desert reaches the borders of Nevada and Arizona in the east, extends south to the Mexican border and beyond, and a narrow piece of it stretches to the northeast beyond the eastern slope of the Sierra Nevada.

There are two deserts, actually: the high **Mojave Desert** to the north, and the lower and more southern **Sonoran Desert**. There are great differences between the two in rainfall, topography and the range and complexity of ecological systems. The two California deserts are actually the western fringe of the massive desert that encompasses the entire southwestern part of the country and continues into Mexico. The California deserts, far from being one flat and uniform block of desolation, are punctuated by sharp, truncated mountain ranges, dry canyons, playas, plateaus, and miles of huge sand dunes creating the impression of an ocean just over the horizon. Streams are usually dry and waterholes very few.

The desert is filled with numerous life forms and communities and each uses ingenious methods to cope with the harsh environment — which is delicately balanced and easily scarred. Life lies patient and dormant in this parched land. After a rainfall, the desert bursts into a profusion of colors and shapes, as flowers open and plants live through their life cycles in accelerated rhythms. Animal life is hard to detect in daylight, but it fills the desert at night, as you see in the morning when the sands are stitched with tracks.

Man penetrated this harsh region at least 12,000 years ago, and as early as 60,000 years ago according to some scholars. Small groups lived by the shores of ancient lakes. As the lakes dried up about 7,000 years ago, the groups became semi-nomadic. In families and clans they wandered the high and low deserts. Strict rules and taboos on relationships and marriage held the groups together in the vastness of the desert. Precursors of the modern Indian tribes left behind huge drawings and petroglyphs (carvings) depicting hunting scenes and creation myths.

Struggles in the desert continue today, but they are not struggles of survival fought by the Indians or by early pioneers crossing and trying to settle the desert. Today the fate of the desert itself is in question.

There are thousands who head for the desert every weekend with dune buggies and other exotic off-the-road vehicles to release their tensions ripping through the sands at Imperial Dunes and other places. For ranchers the desert provides a place to grow winter vegetables under irrigation. Mining companies want to mine gold, gypsum, tungsten and other minerals found in the desert. For the military, the isolation, open space and steady weather provide excellent conditions for field exercises and weapon testing. Environmentalists and scientists want to preserve as much of the delicate desert environment as possible, while archeologists rush to locate and study ancient sites before they are defaced or bulldozed. Chemical companies and other industries which have moved out from the urban area emit noxious clouds into the pristine sky, and energy companies and research firms conduct experiments using geothermal, solar and wind energy (forests of propellered towers can be seen on the way to Palm Springs). Meanwhile, developers and speculators urge the building of more suburban neighborhoods, more shopping centers and more resorts.

Suburban areas have crossed through the passes of the San Bernardino and San Gabriel Mountains, into the western fringes of the Mojave desert, as the urban amoeba of Los Angeles spreads.

Most of the 25 million acres of desert is currently in federal hands and under the jurisdiction of the Bureau of Land Management, which in 1980 formulated a giant regional planning program that designates virtually every inch of this seeming emptiness for some purpose or other. Even today, the various conflicting interest groups are interpreting the results of the huge project, each of course with its own interests and belief at heart.

Today, there is still something foreboding, isolated and wild about the desert. Sprinkled throughout its immensity are escapists and pioneers. Children in some towns still attend one-room school houses, and ranch hands drive a hundred miles for a hoe-down at the general store. Right-wing survivalists and left-wing revolutionaries have hidden and trained here. Cargos of Mexican marijuana are smuggled into clandestine airstrips here. Squatters and hermits, fugitives and religious cultists seek refuge in the desert.

It is still possible, however, for the average traveler to find a pocket of solitude in the desert and wilderness, and to catch a glimpse of a fascinating, primeval world. Those who camp here, either on the roadside or on wilderness trails, will find some sparsely visited yet spectacular landscapes. Even on a one-day visit, the city dweller can enjoy the silence, stillness and elongation of time which is uniquely the desert's.

The fall and the spring are great times for a desert visit. The weather is more moderate, the roads and campgrounds uncrowded. In the spring you can glimpse green hills and valleys that will be parched within a month.

In addition to the largest and best-known desert preserves — Death

Valley National Park, Joshua Trees National Monument and Anza-Borrego Desert State Park — there are smaller parks, some quite remote, featuring some unusual land forms, caverns or hot springs. Other areas are protected by various state or federal agencies, and offer opportunities for fishing, recreational boating, hiking etc. For the tourist, these are likely to be of secondary interest. If by chance you are entering California from Arizona or Nevada, you will cross into the lower desert across the natural boundary of the Colorado River. That once raging water course which carved the Grand Canyon has been tapped and channeled, largely to supply water for Los Angeles and the surrounding area. Several artificial lakes were formed by the damming of the river. The largest is **Lake Havasu** which, since its creation in 1938, has become a recreational center for both Arizona and California. Along 16 miles (25 km) of its shoreline is **Lake Havasu State Park**, which offers a welcome respite for anyone traveling from the east. At **Lake Havasu City**, on the Arizona side, there are many motels and tourist facilities and... the famous **London Bridge**, constructed in 1831 in London and moved block by block to the desert resort town.

The **Providence Mountains State Recreation Area**, off I-40 about 40 miles (65 km) west of the Arizona border, is a popular backpacking area, with its 4,000-foot (1,360 m) high overlooks gazing upon the desert. The **Winding Stairs Cavern** and **Mitchell Caverns** discovered by prospector and homesteader Jack Mitchell in 1929, contain a subterranean garden of stalactites and stalagmites.

Some 12 million acres of public land are administered by the _BLM._ There are some primitive _BLM_ campsites with water, which cost $2 per night. In addition, camping is allowed on these public lands 300 feet (100 m) from any road that is not closed. The _BLM_ lands also include scenic areas. A free recreation guide-map is available from the _BLM_ at 1695 Spruce st., Riverside, 92507.

## Some tips for desert traveling

Population centers and tourist facilities can be few and far between in the desert. Sources of drinking water are limited. Temperatures may shift from 100 degrees Fahrenheit (37 degrees Centigrade) to freezing, within a day. A trip to the desert may require a little thought and planning, but do not let that deter you.

The intensity of the desert sun can be deceptive. Even if you feel fine in the morning, you are losing liquid, up to a gallon a day. In the midst of a pleasant hike you may suddenly be hit by the signs of dehydration — weakness, headaches, dizziness and fatigue. By then, drinking will not help. Drink plenty of water **before** you set out on a walk or car tour, and take plenty with you to drink along the way. Alcohol does not count, as it actually dehydrates the body.

If you are driving through the desert, keep extra water on hand both for drinking and for the radiator. Fill the gas tank when it reaches the halfway mark just to be safe, as the heat and general driving conditions can be a strain on the engine and burn extra fuel.

Wear a broadrimmed hat, sunglasses, protective suncream and layers of loose cotton clothing. In summer as well as winter, bring a sweater for the evenings, which are cool. The desert heat slows your walking pace and makes you feel exhausted, so walk in a relaxed and unstrained rhythm.

Serious accidents involving snakes, scorpions or spiders are rare, but caution is advisable. Don't step on rocks or logs likely to overturn. Don't go prancing around in sandals. At night sleep on a groundcloth, and close your sleeping bag tight if you are not in a tent.

There are ten species of rattlesnakes in California's deserts. Self-treatment for a snake bite should be avoided if a doctor can be reached within two hours. The coyotes that slip like shadows among campsites in the evening are not dangerous; they only want food. They should not be approached, though.

A daily non-stop air service operates between **Palm Desert** and **Los Angeles Airport**. *Air LA* fly three times a day from the **Bermuda Dunes Airport** to the **Imperial Terminal at LAX** for $39 one-way. For more information contact *Air LA* at 6151 W Centary Blvd., Suite 1114, Los Angeles, tel. 213-641-1114, fax 213-641-2344.

The **Imperial Valley College Desert Museum & Information Center** is scheduled to open in 1991. It will occupy 25 acres, 75 miles (120 km) east of San Diego and will focus on paleontology (fossil study), with mammoth, bison and saber-tooth tigers on display, energy development and archeology. Contact California Deserts Tourism Association, P.O. Box 364 Rancho Mirage, LA 92270, tel. 619-328-9256.

# Anza-Borrego Desert State Park

The gigantic Anza-Borrego Desert State Park is about a three-hour drive east of San Diego. It runs almost the entire eastern length of San Diego County from the Mexican border up to Riverside County. The largest state park in the country, it encompasses over two-thirds of all lands in California's extensive state park system. Between the 6,000-foot (2040 m) peaks and the depressions 100 feet (34 m) below sea level near the Salton Sea, lies a vast territory of sculpted desert landscape: bare mountain ridges, steep-cliffed canyons, oases, and bizarre sandstone formations. If you're lucky enough to catch a brief summer downpour you'll witness torrential and transitory waterfalls.

Within this vast desert, the diversity in life is incredible. Hundreds of native plant species range from pines to palms to cactus and to the thick-trunked elephant tree, found only here, north of the Mexican border. In addition to the rare bighorn sheep, for which the park is named (*borrego*, in Spanish), there are mule deer, rarely seen mountain lions, rodents, reptiles and the flocks of birds congregating around the oases.

Over a million visitors a year visit this park. Many come just to witness the explosion of wildflowers, which can begin as early as February in the lower elevations, and which last until June in the higher ones. This park is so huge and varied, however, that even in the crowded season you can find spots to avoid the crowds and can camp virtually alone.

I-8, the super-highway following the Mexican border between San Diego and the Arizona line, runs just below the park boundy. S-22, a much slower, more circuitous route along the northern section of the park off Route 78, offers spectacular views from the western heights. This highway passes through the town of **Borrego Springs**, surrounded by the park, and nearby Borrego Palm Canyon. These two points form the center for park activity.

The cafes and restaurants in Borrego Springs are of reasonable standard but are generally not great bargains. Commodities, not surprisingly, are more expensive than outside the park. Enter the park with as full a gas tank as possible and stock up on food beforehand.

Don't try to see the whole park. Head first for the modern **visitor center**, two miles west of Borrego Springs. The vivid audiovisual presentation as and other exhibits will give some perspective to the size and diversity of the park, and the maps and guidance of the rangers will help you find your bearings and choose which section you want to explore. Excpet durring the summer, the center sponsors, a full schedule of guided walks, campfire programs, lectures and ranger-led car caravans. There are several short, self-guiding nature trails, many spectacular turn-outs and overlooks, and the staff of the visitor center know them all, tel. 767-5311.

There is a very accessible nature trail at **Borrego Palm Canyon**, climbing along a rarely flowing stream into a shady paradise of over 1,000 palm trees. The nearby drive to **Font's Point** leads to a view of the strangely eroded sandstone cliffs of the **Borrego Badlands**.

If you follow S-22 to the east you will descend down the cliffs until you reach the **Salton Sea**, just outside the park boundary and about 230 feet (80 m) below sea level. This is an artificial and accidental lake, caused by an overflow of the Colorado river resulting from channeling. The winter temperatures can be comfortable, between 50-80 degrees Fahrenheit (10-26 degrees Centigrade), but you'll broil in the summer.

About 600 miles (960 km) of roads traverse the hills and flatlands of Anza-Borrego. Besides the main scenic routes are many small dirt roads that penetrate the wilderness. Some are appropriate only for four-wheel vehicles. Check with a ranger about which roads are recommended and accessible.

There are plenty of trails for day hikes and backpacking. Hikers can follow the dirt roads as well. Again, check with a ranger for conditions and specific information. Always drink plenty of water beforehand and take plenty with you. Several canyons in the **Anza-Borrego Desert State Wilderness**, which is in the northwest portion of the park, are very popular with backpackers. The **Pacific Crest Trail** skirts the northwest corner.

## Accommodations

Borrego **Palm Canyon** and **Tamarisk Grove** have well equipped campgrounds. Reservations should be made through *Ticketron*. The others range from less-developed to non-developed and are all on a first-come-first-serve-basis. Anza-Borrego is unique in that camping is allowed anywhere along travel routes, with no payment or permit required. It is easy to find wide open, virtually empty spaces where not one set of headlights will pierce the star-filled night.

Reservations are recommended for the motels found in Borrego Springs. For a listing of local lodgings write to the Chamber of Commerce, Borrego Springs, 92004. El Centero and Smaller Ocotillo, to the southeast of the park along I-8, also have motels. El Centero in the Fertile Imperial Valley has a greater variety.

# Palm Springs

In Palm Springs, the annual Christmas parade is made up of golf-carts and Rolls Royces. The visitor's brochures tell which starlet Howard Hughes signed into a hotel under a pseudonym, which hotel Clark Gable honeymooned in, and what kind of fur stole Joan Crawford wore to ward off the desert chill. The hotel bellhops may wear uniforms designed by Pierre Cardin. Outside air-conditioning keeps revelers cool on the veranda, while using a mere 60 gallons of water per hour. Foreign industrialists fly in their overseas associates for one day of meetings and one night of billiards. It's the place where water is pumped across the desert not to water vegetables, as is done in other countries, but to water golf courses, 70 of them. This is the "golf course capital" of the world, so the locals say, and probably the only spot in the world where politicians and pop stars mingle.

Palm Springs, with its natural hot springs, was once a Cahuilla Indian settlement and burial ground, and then a tiny settlement with a few rail-road workers and some farmers who grew date palms.

With summer temperatures reaching 120 degrees Fahrenheit (48 degrees Centigrade). and powerful winds funneling through the mountain passes in the west, a resort seemed about the last business appropriate here. However, the dryness of the heat, the nearby springs, the privacy, and the advertising campaigns of developers began first to attract movie stars, and then the people who were attracted by the movie stars. Errol Flynn, Greta Garbo, Clark Gable, Spencer Tracy and many others began to visit and then to buy homes here.

Land values soared in the once worthless desert. Following the lead of Palm Springs, the towns of the western Coachella Valley have blended into one glittery resort. Beyond the southern end of Palm Springs, Route 111 has become an endless strip of restaurants, motels and shopping centers.

With the influx of wealthy Whites, the local Indians found themselves in a struggle for survival as great as adaptation to the desert. They managed to regain legal title to their lands, but only after much of it had been built upon. Palm Springs is now laid out in a checkerboard grid of private and Indian ownership. The Cahuillas grant 99-year leases to the hotels and other establishments and collect the rents, while retaining the land they need for themselves.

About a two-hour drive from Los Angeles and slightly longer from San Diego, Palm Springs spreads almost to the eastern slopes of the San Jacinto Mountains. The mountains, with their snow-covered peaks, make a sharp contrast to the desert resort.

One need not be ultra wealthy to enjoy Palm Springs these days, especially during the summer. In contrast to the rest of the state, summer prices here actually drop. The summer here is not for everyone. The basin becomes one huge oven. Your nostrils sting with each breath and the perspiration pours down. You can, however, still enjoy yourself and be active because the heat is so dry. Some of the museums, restuarants and hotels are closed for vacation and repairs; the valley has a quiet, peaceful atmosphere.

## How to get there

**By air:** The Palm Springs Municipal Airport, at the east end of town, is served by regional and California carriers (*Western, Air Cal, American Eagle*) as well as *TWA* and *American Airlines*, thus linking Palm Springs to the main air routes. The airport is just across the road from the *Convention and Visitors Bureau*.

**By land:** The main route to Palm Springs from the Los Angeles region is I-10. From San Diego the most direct freeway route is like an upside-down L: I-15 north, to I-215 northeast, then to Route 60 and I-10 headed east.

*Greyhound* serves Palm Springs, with a terminal downtown. The nearest _Amtrak_ connection is at Indio. From there a _Greyhound_ can be taken to Palm Springs, but it's a tiring trip.

_Desert Stage Lines_ provides daily bus service to Twenty-nine Palms, at the northern edge of Joshua Tree National Monument and Yucca Valley. There are weekend routes to and from L.A. and San Diego.

The _Sun Bus_ provides local transportation. Routes extend throughout the Coachella Valley urban area. Tickets cost 50 cents, with add-ons for crossing into other zones. Operates till 6pm. Buses run downtown very often.

Well-marked bicycle trails are located throughout the city. Bicycle maps are available from the Leisure Services Dept. or from the Visitor Center.

## Accommodations

Palm Springs and the adjacent resort towns spill over with hotels and motels. The reputation for luxurious hotels is well-founded, but nearby there might be that plain old stucco, low-roofed motel with a tiny pool and plastic grass.

Winter and spring are the peak seasons here. Don't go near Palm Springs without advanced reservation. During the roasting summer many hotels close, while many others drop their rates, often by as much as 50%. The _Visitor Center_ and _Chamber of Commerce_ provide a full list of places to stay.

With an abundance of vacation homes in Palm Springs, various rental agencies can arrange for rentals usually by the week or month. This can work out more economically than commercial lodging.

Lodges and cabins are more expensive than "down below", but not out of reach. For lodging information, contact _Associated Idyllwild Rentals_, PO Box 43, Idyllwild 92341, tel. 659-2933. Cheaper but less interesting lodgings are found in Banning and Beaumont on I-10.

Camping can be found about an hour away from Palm Springs, in the desert of Joshua Trees National Monument to the east, or in the state park or national forest campgrounds in the San Jacinto Mountains. The national forest sites are cheaper, and some are free. Check with the forest service in Idyllwild. If you are really exhausted and/or really broke as you drive through the Palm Springs area, there are rest areas on either side of I-10 near the juncture with Route 111, with restrooms. There you will be lulled to sleep by the rumbling of passing trucks.

_Palm Springs Spa_, 100 N. Indian ave., 92262, tel. 325-1461, or 800-472-4371. An opulent and elegant Palm Springs oldie-but-goodie, this five-story hotel captured the town's hot springs. The spa is still the biggest draw. Tennis, and playing arrangements with golf

# *C*ALIFORNIA

## *PALM SPRINGS*

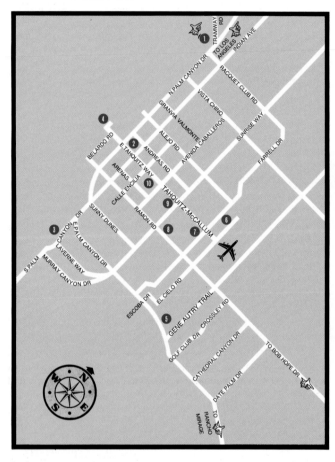

### Index

courses. Prices vary with the season. Singles and Doubles start at $130 in winter, go down to $90 and up in autumn and spring, in the summer they drop to an amazing $45-$70.

*Gene Autry Hotel*, 4200 E. Palm Canyon dr. 92264, tel. 328-1171, toll-free 800-4 Gene Autry in U.S. Another Palm Springs stalwart, 4.5 miles from downtown with balconies, patios and bungalows on beautiful grounds. A fine tennis resort, play arrangements with golf courses. $85 upwards.

For those a bit more modest in requirements or means:

*Villa Royale*, 1620 Indian Trail, tel. 327-2314. A variety of rooms, each done in a different national motif: Dutch, Spanish, English, etc. $55 and up in winter, $49 and up in summer.

*Pepper Tree Inn*, 645 N. Indian ave., tel. 325-9124. A popular and moderately priced B&B, but in a standard motel court setting. Some variety among the rooms. Reservations recommended even in summer. Starting at $49 in winter, $30 in summer.

*Monte Vista Hotel*, 414 N. Palm Canion dr., tel. 325-5641. More standard, more reasonable. Good location. Starts at $35 in winter, $25 in summer.

And, of course, *Motel 6*, tel. 327-4200.

## Food

If you're looking for that cheap little two-bit hole-in-the-wall grease-coated gem of a diner in Palm Springs, forget it; it's long since been bought out. There are diverse restaurants, within a certain range — lots of steak, lobster, Italian, some high-priced delis, with a recent influx of sushi and other oriental food. South of downtown along Route 111 are many more standard cut-out coffeeshops and franchises.

*Aerial Tramway*, at the top of the cable ride, tel. 325-1391. The *Ride & Dine* package, $16.95 (tram tickets alone cost $12.95) includes a nice buffet and unmatchable views.

*Bono*, 1700 N. Indian ave., tel. 322-6200. Well-known for its Italian food and the friendliness of its famous owner, Sonny Bono of the one-time star duo of Sonny & Cher. Dinners $25 up, lunches $6.75 up. Reservation required.

*Las Casuelas*, the original, 368 N. Palm Canyon dr., tel. 325-3213. A local hangout since 1958, this family-operated Mexican restaurant has since opened two branches. The decor is cluttered and colorful, the food is fine, filling and moderate. Crowds at dinner. Lunches start at $4.95, dinners at $10 and up.

*Louise's Pantry*, 124 S. Palm Canyon dr., 325-5124. A good-ole' American counter place, with solid filling breakfasts and meat dinners, great pies, and lines.

# CALIFORNIA

## Tourist sites

People do not visit Palm Springs for serious cultural edification. This is the kingdom where the rich play and the rest play rich. The style here is bright and casual all year round. Ties are rarely called for and orange pants are not confined to the golf course.

If you visit here in the fall or spring you'll want to get out into that open desert air for golf, tennis, jogging, hiking, all those things that healthy people do. In the summer, your main activity will be groping along the pool ledge for your beer.

The many tourist bureaus in Palm Springs and the surrounding resorts will supply you with more information about the place than you ever imagined. The *Chamber of Commerce* and the *Visitors Information Agency* are conveniently located downtown, and the *Convention & Visitors' Bureau* is very near the airport. Two periodicals — *Palm Springs Guide* and the *Desert Arts Calender* — detail events, sites and museums. Cycling maps and lists of restaurants and accommodation with prices are available.

You do not need to stay at a five-star hotel in order to have access to athletic facilities. The **Swim Center** of Palm Springs is open to the public, with recreational swimming starting as early as 6am. For exact schedules, call Tel. 323-8278. The **Visitor Center** can provide a list of golf courses and tennis courts that are open to the public. Some private facilities open their doors to members of clubs from other areas.

**Palm Canyon Drive** is the center of downtown Palm Springs, paralleled by Indian ave. Along these two streets, on either side of Tahquitz ave., are the old established shops and restaurants. They are stylish, chic and expensive. Here, as well as in the newer shopping centers, are the same stores that you find in Beverly Hills. Two early homes — the **McCallum Adobe Museum**, built in 1884, and the **Miss Cornelia White House**, 1983, are found in the Village Green, off South Palm Canyon dr., but these historical restorations are not all that interesting. The external adobe architecture is the most interesting feature here.

The nearby **Palm Springs Desert Museum** (101 Museum dr. off Tahquitz just west of Palm Canyon dr. Open Tues.-Fri. 10am-4pm, Sat.-Sun. 10am-5pm, $4 adults, $2.50 seniors; students, and children with adults free. Free admission the first Tuesday of every month. Closed for about a month before Labor Day, tel. 325-7186). This museum is a good introduction to the land, people, culture and art of the desert. The vivid natural history dioramas reveal the complexity, fragility and variety of desert ecology. The museum has a beautiful collection of Asian art left by the late actor William Holden. An extensive collection of Indian crafts from the American West includes some intricate, finely worked weavings, baskets, rugs and pottery. There are several galleries, a sculpture garden and a theatre for the performing arts. The museum provides good tours, nature walks, films, workshops and all-day ranger-guided hikes.

The most thrilling and worthwhile attraction in Palm Springs is the **Aerial Tramway**. From the foot of the San Jacinto Mountains, the 18-minute climb seems to carry you straight up above the Sonoran desert, revealing wonderful views of the valley. The granite escarpments below are sheer and almost within reach. The steel-girdered towers are anchored on tiny rock shelves with seemingly not an inch to spare. Five separate plant zones pass before your eyes. Reaching the top, at a height of 8,500 feet, you suddenly stand in a world of alpine air, pine forests and snow. This is a completely protected isolated area without cars or roads, the kind of wilderness that people drive for five hours along twisting, ice-covered roads into the Sierras to reach.

The turnoff for the tramway is on Highway 111 about a 15-minute drive from downtown Palm Springs. The first car goes up at 10am, and 8am on weekends. From October to April the last car leaves at 7:30pm, and from May through Labor Day the last one departs at 9pm. Closed for a few weeks after Labor Day. $12.95 round-trip, $7.95 ages 3-12, tel. 325-1391. For snow and ski conditions in winter, tel. 325-4227.

The single outpost of civilization is the chalet-type bar and restaurant at the top of the tram line. The buffet dinner is moderately priced, and the desert views unmatched. The tramway's "Ride & Dine" package is a good deal if you are around after 4pm.

Just past the chalet is a ranger station offering information, maps and regularly scheduled guided walks. Several short trails branch out from here, which lead the hiker into the mountains and still leave him time to catch the tram back down to Palm Springs. In the winter, cross-country skiers ride the tram into the mountains and follow the little-used cross-country trails, while below it may be swimming weather.

**Indian Canyons**, reached by toll road at the end of S. Palm Canyon dr., include several oases with large and very old stands of palms, as well as some spectacular rock formations, hiking and riding trails. Indian handiwork is sold here. The scenery has often appeared in Hollywood movies. Open Oct-May 9am-4pm. Closed in summer. $3.

Desert environments are recreated on large tracts in the **Living Desert Reserve** in Palm Desert, 47900 Portola ave., Palm Desert. Open Sept.-May 9am-5pm. $3.50 adult, $1.50 seniors. On Tuesday free for those under 17. Tel. 346-5694. There are two main walks, one short and one about five miles. Animals can sometimes be spotted pursuing their nightly activities. A special viewing platform allows one to view the desert's nocturnal creatures.

Near Palm Springs are the mineral pools of **Desert Hot Springs**. There are several spas, with prices ranging from $2.50-$4:

*Playing golf at Palm Desert*

*Tropical Motel Spa*: 12962 Palm dr., tel. 329-6610.
*Hot Springs Spa*: 10805 Palm dr., tel. 329-6495.
*Hacienda Riviera Spa*: 67375 Hacienda, tel. 329-7010.

Also in Desert Hot Springs is **Cabot's Old India Pueblo**, 67616 E. Desert View ave. Open daily except Tues. 9:30am-4:30pm. $2, seniors $1.50, ages 5-16 $1, tel. 329-7610. Cabot Yerxa was a genuine desert character, who walked into the valley in 1913 with a quart of water and food in a paper bag, and remained there until his death in 1965. He built a rambling house which was inspired by the pueblos of the Southwest Indians, but became the product of his own imagination. When he started his pueblo he was an isolated settler who walked miles for water and supplies. He scavenged many of the materials, piecing together his maze with cement, scrap lumber, broken glass fashioned into windows, and filling it with Indian and Eskimo artifacts.

## Around Palm Springs

At Indio, to the southeast, the resorts of the Coachella valley taper off and the desert farmland takes over. Here you'll see towering desert palm groves. In Indio, as they say, the fruit doesn't fall far from the tree, and the roadside stands that alternate with the groves offer every variation of a date recipe you can imagine. You can even get

*At the Date Festival*

plain dates. The **Date Festival**, held towards the end of February is a colorful affair with an Arabian theme, and in fact the early farmers gave their towns exotic names such as Sahara. The highlight of the fair is the camel races, but the ostriches aren't bad either.

Route 74 loop brings the motorist through the same contrast of landscapes, from desert floor to snowy peaks, as seen from the aerie tram. Pick up Route 243 south from Banning on I-10, and continue south on Route 74. Or start the route at its southern end, where Route 74 heads south from Route 111, beyond Palm Springs.

At the southern end of the San Jacinto wilderness area is the small mountain resort town of **Idyllwild**, built in contemporary piney-woods. A nice place to stop for a meal or coffee. State Park and National Forest headquarters are located here. A local branch of the University of California, and the **Idyllwild School of Music and the Arts**, with its classes and regularly scheduled summer performances, help make Idyllwild idyllic, tel. 659-2171 for performance schedules.

You know you're not far from Palm Springs when you see the signs for **Hadley's Dates**, and then the huge green dinosaur (named Dinny) lumbering by the highway. Hadley's looks like one of those huge highway discount houses, cleared out and filled with fruits and nuts instead. A great place to browse and munch. Dinny the brontosaurus and his Tyrannasaurus buddy are the creations of the owner of the adjacent Whell Inn. There's a museum in Dinny's belly. For both these stops take the Cabazon exit.

## From Palm Springs to L.A.

The highway from Los Angeles to Palm Springs passes the small city of **Riverside**, which straddles the metropolitan area and the open, rugged desert terrain.

Downtown is the famous **Mission Inn**, a huge historic hotel built in the early California mission style, with turrets, towers and high thick-beamed ceilings, 3649 7th st. Riverside, tel. 714-784-0300. Among the extensive collection of artifacts is a chair used by President Taft, illustrating how big, if not great, the man was.

The almost life-sized figures on the tower clock in the courtyard revolve on the hour. Call before visiting as the hotel has been undergoing renovation.

South of Riverside are the **Glen Ivy Hot Springs**, where you can loosen your tensions as you smear yourself with red clay. True believers are convinced that this mud cleanses the skin of toxins and cures everything from arthritis to acne. In any case it feels great to let yourself bake in it. There are shallow, deep, sunny and shady pools, some with whirlpools. The spa is the favorite hide-away for a growing horde of Glen Ivy groupies. Bring your own bathing suit and towel. Pampering yourself with massages, herbal body wraps and other processes designed to transform your body are extra. Live music is performed on some summer evenings.

Glen Ivy is about an hour's drive from Los Angeles, slightly further from San Diego, and near the main route to Palm Springs. Wend your way to the section of I-15 south of the Riverside Freeway (Route 91). Just a few miles south of that junction you'll come to

Temescal Canyon Road, and from there the signs will lead you to the spa, at 25000 Glen Ivy Road. Admission is a reasonable $9.75 per day, $12.75 on weekends, tel. 714-737-4723.

## Important addresses and phone numbers

Area Code: 619 (in the mountains, some numbers have a 714 area code. These are shown).
Emergency: tel. 911.
Fire and Medical Aid: tel. 327-1441.
Chamber of Commerce: 190 W. Amadao, off Palm Canyon dr., tel. 325-1577.
Palm Strings Convention & Visitors Bureau: 255 N. El Cielo rd., tel. 327-8411. Opposite the airport.
Leisure Services Dept.: tel. 323-8272.
Hiking, Backpacking Information, tel. 327-0222.
_Greyhound_: 311 N. Indian ave, tel. 325-2053.
_Desert Stage Lines_: tel. 367-3581.
_Amtrak_: In Indio, tel. 800-872-7245.
_Sun Bus_: tel. 323-4010.
Hospital: Desert Hospital, tel. 323-6511.

### Public tennis courts:
Ruth Hardy Park: 700 Tamarisk rd. Eight courts, six lighted, no fee.
De Muth Park: 4375 Mesquite ave. Four lighted courts, no fee.

# Joshua Trees National Monument

California's two large deserts, the Mojave and the Sonoran, merge within **Joshua Trees National Monument**, located 50 miles east of Palm Springs. Few areas better illustrate the sharp and subtle contrasts in the vegetation, wildlife and landscape of the two distinct desert systems. Within the compact borders of this shifting desert region, the arroyos, canyons, granite monoliths and steep cliffs create a sharp mosaic, intense in its beauty and delicate in ecological complexity.

The Joshua Trees are abundant at the higher elevations, in the western portion of the park. The tree, a giant yucca, received its common name when Mormons heading west were reminded upon seeing them of Joshua raising his arms as he led his people to the promised land. With a fiery sunset as backdrop, it feels eerie to see a landscape full of twisted, distored human-like silhouettes frozen in a dance around rock domes and outcroppings.

Joshua Trees is usually entered just north of I-10, east of Palm Springs. It is far enough from Palm Springs and the other resort centers to seem wild and isolated, yet close enough for a day's excursion. For a leisurely, unusual drive, approach the park from the forest-covered San Bernardino Mountains. Take Route 38 to Route 18. Follow the meandering curves into the desert below you, and then head southeast on Route 247 to the park itself. The contrast as you wind down from mountain to desert, is stunning.

Like other desert parks, Joshua Trees is difficult to cover without a car. Rentals can be arranged in Palm Springs and Indio. Fill up on gas as there is no fuel in the park.

Public transportation is limited at best. *Desert Stage Lines* runs from Palm Springs to **Twenty-nine Palms**. From there you're on your own.

The **Oasis Visitor Center** (tel. 367-3581). at Twenty-nine Palms features displays that explain the natural and human history of this haunting region. Information is available and the staff are helpful. In the midst of this seeming desolation, the oasis is a haven for birds. A self-guiding nature trail starts here. Ranger-led walks, hikes and campfire talks are offered primarily in spring and fall. Information is posted on the campground bulletin boards, at the Oasis and Cottonwood visitor centers, and at the ranger stations in the park. Drinking water is available only at the facilities at the edge of the park: Cottonwood, Oasis, and Black Rock Canyon.

The main roads penetrate into the park. One axis connects the Oasis Visitor Center in the north with the Cottonwood Visitor Center in the south. Off this splits a road to the northwest, into the rugged high desert. Several dirt roads are open to passenger cars in dry weather. The paved road to **Kets View** climbs the stark Little San Bernardino Mountains, for a beautiful view over the Coachella Valley.

There are trails here for the one-hour walker and the serious desert explorer. The **Cholla Cactus Garden** offers a short loop through a compact juxtaposition of rock formations and desert vegetation. **Pinto Basin**, in the eastern section, is almost entirely wilderness, with trails for experienced and well-equipped desert trekkers. Consult a ranger before beginning a long hike.

In the northwest section of the park, south of the entrance at the town of Joshua Tree, a short nature trail goes through Hidden Valley, a crazy jumble of piled boulders which, according to legend, once sheltered cattle rustlers and stolen herds.

## Accommodations

Joshua Trees has nine campgrounds, but no other lodging. There are campsites for overnight hikers, who should first register at a ranger station. The main center for lodging out of the park is Palm Springs. There are motels in Indio, closer than Palm Springs, and in the little towns to the north: Yucca, Joshua Tree and Twenty-nine Palms. These towns have the usual array of coffee shops as well.

## *DEATH VALLEY*

## Death Valley

Although separated by only 40 miles (64 km), Mount Whitney and Death Valley are worlds apart. Whitney, the highest point in the contiguous United States, towers at about 14,500 feet (4,930 m), while Death Valley, at almost 300 feet (102 m) below sea level, is the lowest point in the western hemisphere.

# CALIFORNIA

**Death Valley National Park** is not all valley, and far from being dead. The valley is ringed by the Panamint Mountains on the west and the Argossa range on the east, with barely a drop of rain breaching the mountain barriers. The lowest spot can be pinpointed at Badwater, 283 feet (96 m) below sea level. From Telescope peak or the other peaks exceeding 10,000 feet (3,400 m), the depression takes on a strange other-worldliness, as does the whole valley at times. Distances become distorted and far-off points shimmer and seem deceptively near. The absolute silence and solitude can make you almost dizzy.

Average rainfall is only two inches per year here, but the number means nothing when a sudden storm breaks and creates violent floods down the slopes and canyons. They are spectacular, but very dangerous. After a flood, the explosion of wild flowers is immediate and fantastic, like the moment when *The Wizard of Oz* turns from black-and-white to color.

In summer average tempertures exceed 115°F (45°C). Even the cooler evenings may reach over 80°F, while mountain slopes are still breezy and pleasant for hiking. A hat is essential and so is plenty of drinking water. Not surprisingly, winter is the most popular season for visitors. Temperatures may hover around 60°F (15°C), but can suddenly drop around 30°F.

Be sure to stock up on food and essentials and to fill the gas tank. Commodities are more expensive within the park than in the outlying towns. Be especially cautious with gasoline. You'll be surprised at how fast the heat, steep roads and general conditions burn fuel, so fill the tank whenever possible. There are only three gas stations in Death Valley: at Scotty's Castle in the north, Stovepipe Wells toward the west, and at Furnace Creek near the center. Keep plenty of water on hand for drinking and the radiator. Stations for radiator water are placed along the road (and marked on many park maps), but remember, this water is not suitable for drinking.

## How to get there

Two main routes lead to Death Valley. From Los Angeles I-15 passes through Barstow on the way to Las Vegas, and route 127 veers north to Death Valley. Many people make a detour to the park coming to or from the gambling center. In my opinion, only rolling down a glacier into a hot spring could cause a greater shock! I-395 runs along the eastern fringe of the Sierras, and near **Lone Pine** (also the turnoff for the approach to Mt. Whitney to the west) Route 136 turns east to the desert reserve. If approaching from the east, Route 178 affords the chance to drive through the southern length of the park. For a fantastic and leisurely detour, take the winding one-way road through Titus Canyon from Route 374 in the northeast (across the Nevada line). Only drivers who feel confident on winding and narrow mountain roads should cross the western mountain passes to **Emigrant** or **Wildrose**. These approaches are higher than those in the east, and open up immense vistas of the scorched basin below.

Access to Death Valley without a car is extremely limited. For bus service write to: *Las Vegas-Tonopah-Reno Stage Line*, 922 E. Stewart ave., Las Vegas, Nevada, 89101, tel. 702-384-1230. *Amtrak* and interstate buses serve Barstow and Las Vegas. Car rentals are available in both cities; reservations are advisable.

## Accommodations

The best private lodging in the park is the *Furnace Creek Inn and Ranch*. It is overpriced at about $150 per couple, and because of limited space, it is usually necessary to book in advance (tel. 619-786-2345). The private portion of Furnace Creek is part amusement park, part shopping center, and is wholly abrasive in the midst of this wilderness. The **Furnace Creek Ranch** is a part of the expensive resort and has nice rooms for $65 and up. A cheaper motel is the **Stove Pipe Weus Village** tel. 786-2387.

The park has nine campgrounds. Three are open all year, the others during particular seasons. Check with rangers for details on roadside and trailside campsites. Overnight hikers must register first, in the Visitor Center in Furnace Creek. Open daily 8am-5pm, tel. 786-2331.

## Tourist sites

Death Valley's main centers at Furnace Creek, Stovepipe Wells and Scotty's Castle can get crowded with people and trailers on holidays and long summer weekends. But there are many small roads and short, easy trails to lure you into the desert. Follow them and you'll discover hidden valleys, canyons and ancient Shoshone Indian rock carvings.

Sooner or later, every visitor passes through **Furnace Creek**, the hub of the park. The **Death Valley Museum** and the **Borax Museum** feature excellent displays on the tenacity and built-in genius of desert life forms, and on the human struggle for survival here, dating back thousands of years. The Visitor Center provides information on trails, off-road camping and desert survival in the summer.

Guided walks and auto caravans are offered in the winter. There are also regular evening programs. The park's private concession, based in Furnace Creek, also offers tours of the Park but for a very high price, starting from about $20 per person.

Easily accessible from Furnace Creek is the loop of **Artist's Drive**, so-named for the broad palette of natural colors. Just north of Artist's Drive is the short **Golden Canyon** interpretive trail, an excellent place to get a feel for this low desert without venturing far from your car. Cautious driving on unpaved **West Side Road**, which parallels Route 178, will take you through some especially rugged and beautiful desert scenery.

**Scotty's Castle** is the best known man-made feature in the park. The elaborate home did not actually belong to "Death Valley Scotty". He persuaded a wealthy and ailing friend from the Midwest to build in Death Valley, and after the death of his friend, Scotty spent the rest of his life living in the castle.

From Emigrant Canyon Road on the west, a road leads to **Wildrose Canyon**, with its row of abandoned charcoal kilns, constructed more than a century ago. Even in this barren wilderness, patterns of modern society held sway; the kilns were built by Chinese laborers and tended by Shoshone Indians. Beyond the kilns, at the Mahogany Flat Campground, is the trailhead for the hike to **Telescope Peak**, the highest spot in the park, offering a panoramic view across the sunken valley. Plan on a strenuous all-day hike to the summit. Once there, you'll find a stand of bristlecone pines. Although the age of these particular trees is not known, they belong to the oldest living species on earth. Examples of such trees in the White Mountains to the north are estimated to be 4,000 years old.

## Around Death Valley

Facilities are cheaper in the little towns along the approaches to Death Valley. Most of the motels are of the usual cardboard cut-out variety. It is wise to check the room first. The *Little Lake Hotel* in Little Lake, on I-395 about 25 miles (40 km) south of the 190 turnoff to Death Valley, is clean and friendly and has more character than many others. If approaching from I-15, try the *Armagosa Hotel* in Death Valley Junction (Armagosa), at the junction of Route 127 and 190, just east of the entrance to the park. For an unexpected bubble of culture, visit the **Armagosa Opera**, which has shows of dance and mime. Call the 619 operator and ask for Death Valley Junction no. 8.

# Las Vegas

If you drive through the desert toward Las Vegas at night, it appears suddenly like a psychodelic Emerald City, and, on a closer approach, the dazzling waves of light only appear more surreal. The city's strip, sometimes known as Las Vegas boulevard, never closes. People stand glued to the slot machines and computerized games. Old ladies dressed up like teenagers guard their spots jealously. The lights keep flashing and the money keeps flowing, most of it in one direction. The official euphemism for gambling is 'gaming'.

The biggest hotels and casinos and half of Nevada's population are

*Surrealistic Las Vegas*

found in Las Vegas. Lodging and food are incredibly cheap, which is part of the attraction, but these gains are all evened-out in the casinos.

## Transportation

**By air: McCarran Airport**, at the southern end of the strip, is served by major national carriers.

**By land:** Las Vegas is easy to reach. Along I-15 from Los Angeles it is a five or six hour drive through the Mojave Desert. Bus tours called *Gamblers' Specials* leave L.A. frequently, usually early in the morning, returning late at night or the following day. They range from $5-$10 but, on special offer, may cost as little as $1. Tourist information centers, hotels and travel agents can provide details. *Greyhound*, *Trailways* and *Amtrak* all reach Las Vegas from L.A., but their prices are higher than the *"Gamblers' Special"*.

Besides gambling and other forms of sin, the main activities in Las Vegas are wandering through the streets and gazing at the people playing the machines, eating, watching spectacular shows and trying out the downtown bars and discos.

The major hotels with casinos include the *Aladdin, Caesar's Palace, Circus Circus, The Dunes, MGM Grand Hotel,* and *Del Webb's*

*Sahara.* They stage spectacular shows, featuring some of the biggest names in show business. Dinner and a show in these hotels can run up a hefty bill.

## Accommodations

Accommodation is easy to find. The best deals may be as low as $10, both during the week and on weekends. The buffet breakfasts, lunches and dinners are famous. Off the strip, in downtown, there are many restaurants, not quite the bargains of the casino restaurants, but still excellent.

Check through the various brochures found at the local Visitors' Center (which is right off the strip) and at the casinos and hotels, to find out about special discounts, dinner specials etc. Many motels, as a matter of course, offer guests coupons for breakfast, gambling, complimentary drinks, etc. As long as you keep control of your wallet, Las Vegas can provide an entertaining, dazzling and inexpensive excursion, but if you do not join in the search for El Dorado, the glitter and novelty soon wear thin.

From Las Vegas, it is an easy trip to the imposing **Hoover Dam**, which created **Lake Mead** when the Colorado River was dammed. *Grayline* runs tours to Hoover Dam.

## Important addresses and phone numbers

Emergency: tel. 911.
Area Code: tel. 702.
Las Vegas Convention and Visitors Authority: At the Convention Center, 3150 Paradise rd., tel. 733-2323.
*Greyhound:* 3000 Las Vegas blvd. (at the *Stardust Hotel* on the strip), tel. 734-6961. Also 200 Main st., tel. 382-2640. Open 24-hours.
*Trailways:* 217 4th st., tel. 385-1411.
*Amtrak:* 1 N. Main st., tel. 384-3540. Buses run very frequently along the strip.

# Los Angeles

Los Angeles is a huge metropolis buzzing day and night, conventional but always offering something new, with a constant bombardment of audiovisual electronic stimuli. It is a city which typifies futuristic America — for better or worse. L.A. is the new Ellis Island, but the huddled masses arrive not in rotting freighters but by 747, and they are greeted not by the Statue of Liberty but by air like pea soup.

L.A. is a city of many faces...two-bit conmen...an old Chinese man in the snack-bar of a gigantic discount store, eating a hot dog and tortilla chips with a Sony Walkman over his Dodger's cap...a young blonde man in a three-piece suit wearing an earring.

L.A. means freeway hypnosis and palm trees silhouetted against a green sunset. Here imitation itself becomes the new culture, with false-fronted replicas of quaint fishing villages and frontier towns. Trendy new 1950's style rock'n roll diners are complete with spinning stools, Elvis posters — and a Filipino manager shouting "cheese burger, fries and strawberry shake — hold the mayo!". Tanning salons are crowded even when the sun is shining, and driveways are lined with marble pillars.

L.A., "the city you love to hate", has become the city I hate to love, but do.

Los Angeles is the name of a city, a county and the basin which embraces them. The basin is surrounded by several mountain ranges which arch from the southeast to the northwest. A long mountainous ridge north of the basin stretches toward the Pacific, and to the south, the Palos Verdes Peninsula thrusts out like a hammerhead. Between these two points lie the long, straight Los Angeles beaches. South of the city are the twin ports of Los Angeles and Long Beach.

The basin is roughly 75 miles from north to south, and 70 miles from east to west. Once rich agricultural land, almost every inch has been transformed into housing tracts, swimming pools, malls and shopping centers, freeways, parking lots and wide streets lined with fast-food joints. This urban development continues to spread, creeping over every mountain pass into the desert, and along the coast in both directions. It reaches and lends its name and culture to a territory far exceeding that of the Los Angeles basin itself.

Somewhere in the midst of this endless grid is the city of Los

## *LOS ANGELES AND VICINITY*

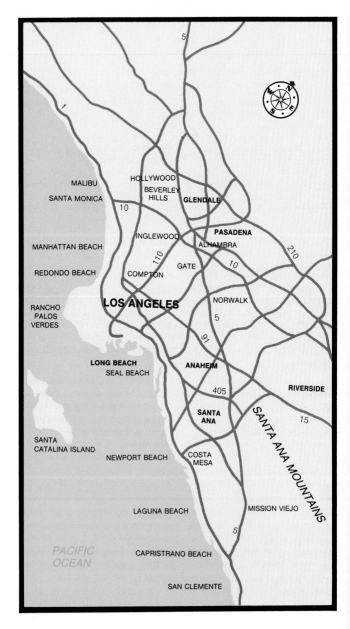

Angeles itself, which covers but a small section of the basin. Scan a map for the largest tangle of converging freeways: the 5, 10, 101 and 110. There you will find original downtown Los Angeles. From here, the city expanded west through Hollywood, Beverly Hills, and West Hollywood to the bluffs and beaches of Santa Monica and Malibu.

Amazingly, this gargantuan urban area is still surrounded by large tracts of undeveloped land. The mountains are dotted with small towns, summer homes, ski resorts, man-made lakes, state parks, trails, and campgrounds. You can easily ski and swim on the same day in the L.A. area, if you can push through the traffic. The highest peak in the region, **Mt. Baldy** in the San Gabriel range, is over 10,000 feet (3,400 m) high, and is visible on a clear day even from the southern edge of the basin, near Long Beach. The beaches extend from Zuma in the north, south to the beaches of Orange County; wide, flat, and almost uninterrupted.

But pristine days are becoming rare. Even with stringent restrictions against pollution enforced in recent years, L.A. continues to be plagued by a serious smog problem, and summer "smog alert" days are all too common and are now part of the local vernacular and thinking.

The same features which make L.A. a unique and desirable region also contribute to that brown smog hovering over it all. The ocean winds, blowing east, push industrial fumes into the basin, where they are trapped by the mountains. The higher warm air currents trap the poorly ventilated layer of pollutants below. It is estimated that up to 65% of the pollution in the area is caused by automobiles, but L.A.'s love affair with, and dependence on, the automobile are irreversible.

## Climate

The weather is extremely mild and pleasant, day after day after day. There's hardly a breeze in the air or a cloud in the sky. For the traveler, it makes packing easy. A light jacket, heavy sweater and raincoat are usually adequate year round. When the temperature dips below 45°f (7°C), the locals take out their designer down vests. Dramatic weather changes do occur over the years — the average rainfall of 14 inches may, in reality, indicate 25 inches one year and 3 the next.

The weather varies more from place to place than by season. The temperature along the beaches can be 10-20 degrees cooler than inland, and the winds strong enough to dispel the smog. The inland San Fernando and Gabriel Valleys are generally hotter in summer and colder in winter than the coast. Spring can be cool and foggy along the beaches, while inland the temperatures are fair and the skies clear. The summers can be hot and choking with smog, though it is generally less noticeable along the coast where the sea breeze circulates. The inland communities, such as Riverside, are stuck with the brown smog blown in from the west. Do not expect the crisp autumn of New England, with its vague scent of rotting apples. There's hardly a deciduous tree to turn color. Here, fall is the season of the Santa Annas, the scorching, dry winds from the desert, similar to Mediterranean sirocco winds.

The sunny, warm weather and the openness of L.A. society, lend themselves to a casual and bright clothing style. Jackets and ties are not often necessary at restaurants. In certain occupations it is quite acceptable to wear a sports jacket without a tie. Men's clothing tends to be brighter and lighter in color than on the east coast.

## Orientation

Very few neighborhoods in Los Angeles are clearly demarcated or defined. Downtown lies with the square roughly formed by the Hollywood Freeway (101), the Santa Monica Freeway (10), the Harbor Freeway (11) and the Golden State Freeway (5). To the northeast is Pasadena, anchored at the base of the San Gabriel Mountains, and to the southwest is Exposition Park with its museums. To the northwest are Griffith Park, Hollywood and West Hollywood, all bordered on the north by the Santa Monica Mountains. To the west, beyond Hollywood, lies Beverly Hills, and the Westwood Village/UCLA area. Wilshire Boulevard extends due west from downtown, through a variety of neighborhoods, past the museums and tarpits of Hancock Park through Beverly Hills, into Westwood and out to Santa Monica. Santa Monica is the main beach community west of downtown. To the north lie the hills and curving coast of Malibu. To the south lies the funky ocean walk of Venice, the huge pleasure boat harbor of Marina Del Ray, the airport, and a series of beach neighborhoods leading to the jutting Palos Verdes Peninsula. To the east of the peninsula lies the port of Los Angeles, and the city of Long Beach. Orange County begins south of Long Beach.

A glance at the map will suffice to show that these areas form only a portion of the Los Angeles urban area. The remainder of that huge territory is filled with endless tracts of houses and shopping centers. There may be some tourist sights scattered among them, but most places of interest are concentrated in the areas mentioned, mainly from downtown toward the west.

The less often you need to board a bus or climb into your car, the happier your day will be. Distances between or even within neighborhoods are greater than they seem on a map. If you can plan your excursions so that you spend, for example, one day in the Venice/Santa Monica/Malibu region, you will find your visits more enjoyable. During rush hours — which seem to get longer every year — traffic can be brutal. The best way to handle the rush hour is simply to stay in one place, off the roads.

Los Angeles can overwhelm the most intrepid explorer. It is highly recommended to make a bee-line for downtown and the **Los Angeles Visitors and Convention Bureau**, Manalife Plaza, 11th floor, 515 S Figueroa st., tel. 213-624-7300, fax 213-624-9146. The staff here are patient and helpful and have seen their share of confused visitors. Help is available in a variety of languages. Brochures are abundant. *The Dateline*, published four times a year, lists special events. Many of the brochures include coupons for assorted discounts. A listing of accommodation is available and the staff will help you choose a place best suited to your needs.

There is an amazing amount to do in Los Angeles. Every type of entertainment and culture seems to prosper in the southern Californian sun and freedom. First-run movies are shown everywhere. There are 150 local theaters. From classical to jazz, from folk, country and western to hard rock and punk, the best of every kind of music can be found. Museums and galleries are constantly presenting new exhibits. However long you stay in the area, there is enough to keep you busy day and night.

An excellent array of weekly publications keeps the visitor informed of various happenings. The *L.A. Weekly* and *The Reader* are both free and are geared towards younger audiences, with reviews of rock groups and so forth, but with plenty of general information. They also carry some local investigative articles. The two main daily papers, the *Los Angeles Times* and the *Los Angeles Examiner*, both publish Sunday editions with cultural events and schedules. *The Times* is generally considered one of the best papers in the country. The thick Sunday edition will hold your attention right through Sunday brunch and endless cups of coffee.

In addition, there is a flurry of small neighborhood papers that deal mostly with local matters, which can be interesting. They can be found in restaurants, laundromats and coffee shops.

## Phones

The area code for most of L.A. is 213. In the northern part, including the San Fernando Valley, a new code of 818 was recently introduced. In Orange County the number is 714. All the numbers that have been listed here are under the 213 area code, unless otherwise noted. The basic price of a public phone call is 25 cents, with additional coins required when indicated by the operator.

## Transportation

**Los Angeles International Airport (LAX)** is huge, being the third busiest airport in the world. From the adjacent freeway a wide half-circle of jetliners can be seen hovering in the haze, each awaiting its chance to land, in an endless precise succession.

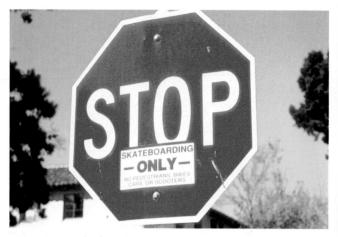

*Skateboarding only in California*

Once dangerously chaotic, the airport is now well-organized after extensive renovations. It is shaped like a long, double-tiered horseshoe, the upper tier for departures and the lower for arrivals. In the central space are parking structures, and a tower with a well-reputed restaurant on top. Concrete islands for all buses, vans and other airport transportation are found outside the lower tier, in front of the luggage carousels. The horseshoe is divided into nine terminals which are connected by shuttle buses. At its curved end is the **International Terminal**, though many international airlines operate out of **Terminal 2** as well. Between the two, LAX handles flights to and from the entire world.

The newly streamlined airport still has a hazardous and hopelessly inadequate entrance. Basically, one road leads to the airport from the San Diego Freeway, and the lane which leads to the airport is regularly jammed with traffic. Be sure to give yourself adequate time to reach the airport. Arrival by bus or van, though it might be an extra expense, may prevent headaches.

The airport has a well-developed information network. For general information on current carriers, airline location, etc. call Tel. 646-5252.

Yellow courtesy phones are available in all terminals and connect you to the airport information aides, who are on duty from 7am-11:30pm. There is a central visitor information number and a number just for transportation information. Each terminal offers Travelers Aid information, with an attendant or recorded information and printed information. For the extremely rumpled, there are showers and sleeping facilities in the International Terminal, which are paid for by the hour.

The central parking structures are convenient but can get crowded, and are expensive for any period exceeding two hours or so. "Remote lots" are cheaper and help one to avoid the snarl of traffic at the terminals. Lots C and D at Sepulveda and 96th and lot VSP at La Cienega and 111th are connected to the airport by free tram. The first two hours at these lots are free. At lot C, a special mini-van provides free service to passengers in wheelchairs.

Public buses (RTD) serve the airport but do not enter it directly. They stop at the **transfer terminal** at Vicksburg and 96th, and the RTD shuttle (3608) scurries between the transfer point and the airport terminals, from 5am-1am. Transfers for the shuttle are also free for those who come to the airport by city bus. In either direction, remember to request a transfer.

Bear in mind that city buses have little or no luggage space and no attendant to leap down and help you. Depending on the hour, the bus might be crowded and the ride drawn-out. You might have to wait for the shuttle and for the connecting city bus. Consider whether this is worthwhile after a long flight.

A more expensive but faster and infinitely more convenient alternative is provided by **Airport Service**, a private company running buses from the airport to various destinations in the basin. They run to the various hotel districts, to downtown, to Pasadena, and to the airports in Long Beach and Orange County, as well as to Disneyland. Another popular way to get to the airport is with the **supershuttle**, tel. 213-417-8988. A van that holds up to seven passengers will pick you up from your door to the airport for $10-15. In addition, there is a wide array of vans and limousines providing direct connections from LAX to regions as far away as Santa Barbara and San Diego. Information is available at the airport.

Car rental counters are available at every terminal. Taxi fares are steep, about $30 to downtown.

Each terminal has phones connecting directly to specific hotels. The closest hotel district that does not gaze over a parking lot is at nearby Marina Del Ray, with a sheltered beach and the largest man-made pleasure-craft marina in the world. Hotels here range from upper moderate to deluxe, and most of the large chains are represented.

### Airport Information

LAX, main number: tel. 646-5252.
Visitor Information (multilingual): tel. 488-9100.
Transportation, parking information: dial AIRPORT.
Travelers Aid: In all terminals, with live information or a recorded

message, and printed material, tel. 646-2270.
Services for the handicapped: tel. 646-8021, or 646-6402.
Lost & Found: tel. 646-2260 (also call the airline).

**Airport Service Buses**:
Los Angeles: tel. 723-4636.
Long Beach: tel. 596-1662.
Orange County: tel.714-776-9210.

# Public transportation

**Buses and trains:** Greyhound, Trailways, and the Green Tortoise (the alternative inexpensive bus company with bunks in the bus) all serve Los Angeles, with connections to most major cities. The Greyhound station is in skid row; try to avoid it late at night. Trailways is located in the beautiful Union Station which is also used by Amtrak. Today, only a few trains a day pass through it as part of the beautiful coastal route.

## The freeways

Mass hypnosis captures Los Angeles every morning as people, half-asleep climb into their cars, rev the motor, turn up the radio and air conditioner, and squeeze into the morning crawl of traffic on the nearest freeway. On every freeway in the complex network, cars are packed tight from horizon to horizon. It is impossible to imagine Los Angeles today without the freeway system. It is common for people to commute up to a hundred miles (160 km) each day. The traffic never really lets up beyond a certain point. At five in the morning traffic already streams toward the city.

The afternoon rush hour may begin before three and continue well after six. During these peak hours the surface streets which parallel the main freeways often move faster than the freeways which were built to bypass the surface streets.

The Los Angeles freeways can disconcert the unfamiliar driver. Be cautious when entering the freeway. Some ramps serve as exits and entrances, inviting accidents.

Yield to the driver already on the freeway, but try not to stop and break the flow of traffic behind you. Ease gently into the flow. Beware of tailgating; chain-reaction pile-ups can occur in a flash. Ignore those who get their kicks weaving between lanes. Shift lanes sparingly as long as the traffic is flowing.

The Santa Monica Freeway 10, is the main east-west axis from downtown to the western beaches. Paralleling the coastal areas, from the northern San Fernando Valley all the way south to San Diego is the San Diego Freeway 405, becoming Freeway 5 in Orange County. These two roads draw some of the heaviest congestion. From Hollywood to downtown take the Hollywood Freeway 101. Between downtown and the harbor area take the Harbor Freeway 110. These four freeways link up with almost every other one in the complex.

# In-town transportation

**Buses:** Contrary to popular rumor, Los Angeles has an extensive public bus system. It is, however, complicated, involving interchanges and crossovers between the *Southern California Rapid Transit District* (*RTD*) and other local and regional bus lines. Buses often follow long, indirect routes through city streets, and may run well over half-an-hour apart even during peak hours. A trip including a transfer between buses may require two hours.

RTD's **customer centers** throughout the urban area, including one downtown (see below), can provide all the necessary information, as well as schedules and various passes. Information is available by phone from 6am to midnight, but the wait can be excruciatingly long. A visit to the nearest customer center is preferable, if possible.

When obtaining bus information, be sure to ask about express routes (following the freeway or a combination of freeway and street). Unless you specify, you might receive information concerning the stop-and-go street routes only. Express buses are much faster than the street routes.

Basic fare is $1.10, 55 cents for handicapped and seniors. Transfers are 25 cents. Express routes cost an additional fare, depending on distance. Monthly passes for unlimited use cost $42.

*RTD* runs three shuttles: the Westwood Village Shuttle, the downtown shuttle and the airport shuttle (each is detailed under those subtitles).

Buses run till the wee hours and some run all night. It is best to avoid the *Greyhound* bus terminal (which is also the downtown hub for *RTD*) and environs late at night if possible.

A written request to *RTD* will get you enough information to fill a suitcase. A brochure for self-guided tours is offered, as is information for routes in specific areas, and a guide to wheelchair accessible lines. Write: *RTD*, Los Angeles 90001.

Some of the same destinations in the L.A. area served by RTD and other public bus companies are also served by *Greyhound* and/or *Trailways*. These lines are more expensive, but save time and are more convenient.

## Transportation Information

*Amtrak*: Union Station, 800 N. Alameda, tel. 624-0171.
*Greyhound*: 208 E. 6th st. & Los Angeles, tel. 620-1200.
*Grayline Sightseeing Tours*: tel. 680-1980.

*Green Tortoise*: tel. 415-285-2441.
*RTD*: tel. 626-4455. Service is faster if called from an RTD customer center.

## RTD Customer Centers:

Manulife Plaza: 515 S. Figueroa st., 11th floor. Mon.-Fri. 7:30am-4pm.
Hollywood: 6249 Hollywood blvd. Mon.-Sat. 10am-6pm.
Main Office: 419 S. Main. Mon.-Fri. 8am-4:30pm.
The California Mart: 1016 S. Main. Mon.-Fri. 7am-7pm, Sat.-Sun. 10am-6pm.
Wilshire (temporary): 5315 Wilshire blvd., just west of La Brea ave., Mon.-Fri. 8am-5pm.

## Accommodations

Most of the hotels and motels in the Los Angeles area are modern structures, some ultra modern sky-scrapers. The major chains, both of motels and hotels, are well represented in most major tourist areas. They are spread throughout the city, but the main areas are Marina Del Ray, Beverly Hills, West Los Angeles and Santa Monica. These areas are generally more expensive.

The downtown area may be less expensive, as it is not yet very fashionable, although it has been largely renovated. West of Broadway there are many hotels and motels to choose from. Here there are some older and more moderately priced hotels, as well as luxurious ones. The major information centers are found in this area.

### Very expensive

*New Otani Hotel & Garden*: Downtown, 120 S. Los Angeles st., L.A. 90012, tel. 629-1200. U.S. toll-free 800-421-8795, toll-free CA 800-252-0197. A world class, luxurious hotel. Some rooms are centered around the Japanese garden, as are the bar and several restaurants. Located in Little Tokyo. Airport service.

*Biltmore Hotel*: Downtown, 506 S. Grand st., L.A. 90071, tel. 624-1011 or 800-421-8000. A refurbished red-brick downtown hotel, with a Spanish lobby of marble and intricately hand painted ceilings. Its bar is popular, its coffee shop reasonable and its French restaurant, *Bernard's*, an expensive L.A. classic. Place for the rich and famous.

*L'Ermitage Hotel*: Beverly Hills, 2921 Burton Way 90201, tel. 278-3344 or 800-424-4443. One of the best hotels in the west coast. Modern facilities with plenty of charm.

### Expensive

*Ambassador*: Willshire, 3400 Willshire blvd., 90010, tel. 387-7011, 800-421-0182. Very good atmosphere in this 1920s hotel. Good location and interesting decoration.

**Moderate**

*Figueroa Hotel:* Downtown, 939 S. Figueroa st., L.A. 90015, tel. 627-8971, 800-421-9092 or toll-free CA 800-331-5151. Spanish style, comfortable rooms, old-fashioned bathrooms. Near the Convention Center. Airport service and other amenities. $48-$58 single, $58-$64 double.

*Rainbow Hotel:* 536 S. Hope st. L.A. 90071, tel. 627-9941 or 800-435-9153. In the heart of downtown, recently renovated, a popular and recommended moderately priced hotel. $44 up single, $50 up double. Near airport bus.

**Inexpensive**

*Hotel Carver:* Downtown, 460 E. 4th st. L.A. 90013, tel. 972-9228. A clean, friendly inexpensive little hotel in Little Tokyo. Many Japanese guests. $15-20 single, $30-$36 double.

*Courtesy Inn:* Hollywood, 2011 N. Highland ave., tel. 851-1800. Basic but clean rooms in the center of Hollywood. Near the Hollywood Bowl.

*Carmel Hotel:* Santa Monica, 201 Broadway, 90401, tel. 451-2469. Close to beach and shopping centers. Very good hotel for low budget travelers who wish to stay a week or more in L.A.

There are several American Youth Hostel facilities in the metropolitan L.A. area. None are right downtown, but most have access to public transportation and the staff know the bus routes. Most cost $6-$8 for members, and slightly more for non-members.

*Hollywood Hostel:* 1553 N. Hudson ave., tel. 467-4161. Often crowded. Located in the *Hollywood YMCA*, which also offers rooms and is also crowded, tel. 467-4161.

*Bill Baker International Youth Hostel:* Westchester YMCA, 8015 S. Sepulveda blvd., tel. 776-0922. Near the airport.

*Los Angeles International Youth Hostel:* 1502 Palos Verdes dr. N., Harbor City, tel. 831-8109. Near the Palos Verdes Peninsula and Long Beach.

*Huntington Beach Colonial Inn Hostel:* 421 8th st., Huntington Beach, tel. 536-3315. One of the most pleasant in the area, near the beach, in an old house.

*Venice Beach Hotel:* 25 Windward ave., tel. 399-7649. Very friendly, but a little noisy. Good rooms. More expensive than the other hostels.

# Food
**Downtown**

*The Far East Cafe:* 347 E. 1st st. A great Chinese restaurant found at the edge of Little Tokyo. With its original wooden booths and deep interior, this is the place you'd come to for a secret assignation. The detective film *Farewell My Lovely* included scenes shot here. The lunches are good and filling, under $5.

*The Biltmore Bar.* 515 S. Olive st. In the beautifully renovated red-brick hotel, a relaxing and popular place to wet the whistle. The *Biltmore Coffee Shop* offers the standard fare at reasonable prices.

*The Grand Central Public Market*: 317 S. Broadway. This bazaar is a sight in itself (see "Downtown").

*Vickman's*: 1228 E. 8th. Opening at 3am, this is one of the best-known restaurants catering to the early morning produce workers. Fresh bakery.

*The Pantry Cafe*: 877 S. Figueroa st. Open 24 hours, and busy for most of those, serving steak, sourdough and hashbrowns, in the same way since 1924.

*Cafe Pasquini*: 701 W. 7th. Antipasto, pasta, expresso, sunlight and European ambience. Breakfast and lunch.

*Clifton's Cafetaria*: 648 S. Broadway. An original cafeteria, from 1912. No waiting, great variety, great prices, great show on the walls and maybe at the next table. Kitsch raised to an art.

## Hollywood

Along Hollywood boulevard, and in the surrounding area, you can find classic Hollywood restaurants, reasonable ethnic restaurants and fast food stands.

*Musso and Frank Grill*: 6667 Hollywood blvd., tel. 467-7788. An overpriced but classic Hollywood establishment dating back to 1919.

*C.C. Brown's*: 7007 Hollywood blvd. The decor of this ice-cream parlor is from the 1920s, the prices from the 1980s. They claim to have invented the hot fudge sundae, and they do indeed serve a great fudge.

*Addis Ababa*: 6263 Leland Way, tel. 463-9788. Ethiopian cuisine presented in a converted house near the corner of Vine St. Very warm and homey, with small rooms available. A delicious vegetarian dinner served on *injira* (Ethiopian bread) starts at $4.95.

*Orean: The Health Express*: 1320 N. Vine, tel. 462-9945. Simply fantastic for anyone wanting the service and price of a fast-food stand but concerned about health. All their food is vegetarian, including soy burgers and bran pancakes. Tables are of polished wood and ferns decorate the interior. There is a great menu which contains information about famous vegetarians and vegetarianism, plus a quote from George Bernard Shaw: "Animals are my friends...and I don't eat my friends."

*Seafood Bay*: 3916 blvd., tel. 664-3902. Crowded and extremely popular. The food is delicious and reasonably priced.

*Cantor's Fairfax Restaurant Delicatessen and Bakery*: 419 N. Fairfax ave., tel. 651-2030. Open 24 hours a day, often frequented by Hollywood stars. Tremendous variety on the menu.

*Tex Mex Cafe*: 1108 N. Flores st. West Hollywood. Chic, cool and pleasant with a shaded patio. Serves huge portions of delicious non-greasy Mexican food. A deep dish tostada is big enough for two.

*The Tail of the Pup*: 311 N. La Cienaga, across from the Beverly Center. The ultimate hot-dog stand. It has been featured in several films.

*The Egg and the Eye*: 5814 Wilshire blvd., on the balcony of the Craft and Folk Museum. In keeping with the surrounding motif, you can create your own omelette.

**Beverly Hills**
*Lawry's*: 55 N. La Cienaga, tel. 652-2827. Serving moderately priced ribs, ribs and more ribs. People wait in line to get in.

**Santa Monica**
*Pioneer Boulangerie*: 2102 Main st. A bakery, cafetaria and restaurant. A popular local spot.

*Cafe Casino*: Arizona and Ocean Park. A Mediterranean style outdoor cafe with cafeteria prices. Refreshing breeze from the sea across the street and foreign languages spoken all round.

*Todai*: Arizona and 2nd. All you can eat for $10, and delicious too.

*Charmer's Market*: 180 Pier ave. A combined delicatessen and restaurant, specializing in imported and exotic delicacies for the gourmet.

# Entertainment
An endless variety of entertainment keeps Los Angeles alive and vibrant all the time. Concerts range from classical to punk. There are night clubs, dinner clubs, dancing clubs and comedy clubs. Everyone who wants to make it in the entertainment world tries their luck out here. Consequently, there is an enormous variety and range in the quality of the entertainment. The local papers and weekly guides keep up to date with current performances.

Classical: **Dorothy Chandler Pavilion** in the music center, 135 N. Grand ave., tel. 972-7211, is the home of the **L.A. Philharmonic**, as well as the **Opera**, **Joffrey Ballet** etc. Other performers can be seen at the **Hollywood Bowl**, tel. 850-2000, and in the **Ambassador Auditorium** in Pasadena, tel. 818-304-6161. In **UCLA** you may catch a good concert in the **Royce Hall** or the **Schoenberg Hall**, tel. 825-9261.

If you want to catch a uniquely Los Angeles aspect of entertainment, check out some of the comedy clubs. Los Angeles is obviously a major center for aspiring comics. In the last few years, the number of clubs concentrating solely on comedians has grown. Most of these have some sort of amateur night, in which unknown aspiring artists have a chance to show their talent. Occasionally some famous "graduates" of a particular comedy club return to check out the hopefuls or to polish their own acts. These amateur or showcase nights offer a glimpse of the inner workings of show business, and some of the performers are incredible.

*Comedy Store*: 8433 Sunset blvd., W. Hollywood, tel 656-6225. One of the earliest of the comedy clubs here, it has grown to a three-room operation, each with a different focus.

*The Improvisation*: 8162 Melrose ave., W. Hollywood, tel. 651-2583. Another comedy institution, presenting both stand-up comics and improvisational theater.

*The Laugh Factory*: 8001 Sunset blvd., Sunset blvd., W. Hollywood. Small, more recent and more intimate than the others. The level of talent may be more variable.

*Comeback Inn*: 1633 W. Washington blvd. in Venice, tel. 396-7255. A different kind of music every night. Mostly jazz, crowded on Saturday nights.

*The Troubador*: 9081 Santa Monica blvd., W. Hollywood, tel. 276-6168. Famous as the launching pad for a number of rock stars, such as Elton John, James Taylor, and Linda Ronstadt. During the week acts range from country-rock to post new wave, and weekends feature bigger talent, with occasional famous drop-ins such as Bob Dylan.

*Mischa's*: 7561 Sunset blvd, Hollywood, tel. 874-3467. A gaudy, colorful, tent-covered Russian style cabaret, kitschy and fun, featuring many famous Russian immigrant entertainers.

# What to See

## Downtown

L.A. really does have a downtown and it can be fascinating, but you must hunt out its interesting and eccentric corners. Downtown L.A. is roughly oblong, and runs approximately from Chinatown in the north to the Santa Monica freeway in the south. It is a composite of several sections: the financial district, the small ethnic communities and tourist centers (Chinatown, Little Tokyo, Olvera St.), the commercial wholesale areas, and skid row around the *Greyhound* Station.

# *C*ALIFORNIA

## *DOWNTOWN LOS ANGELES*

### Index

The downtown minibus, called *DASH*, Connects Olvera St., Little Tokyo, Chinatown, City Hall, The World Trade Center, ARCO Plaza, and other downtown points, as far south as the Trans America Center on 12th St. It also passes produce markets on the eastern edge. The buses run every 10 minutes or so, from 7am to 6pm, but sometimes they arrive up to 20 minutes apart. Most main attractions are on this convenient line which costs only 25 cents, tel. 800-8–SHUTTLE.

The **ARCO Plaza**, at 6th st. and S. Flower, is a logical place to begin a downtown tour. The seven acres of this underground world might be the prototype for futuristic cities; quiet with pumped-in air, dim lights, pleasant music and almost hermetically sealed from obtrusive outside noises. It is gleaming, spotless and bland. Just around the corner, the **RTD Customer Center** is offering information schedules. The **ARCO Center for Visual Art**, open Mon.-Fri. 10am-6pm, Sat. 11am-5pm. Free admission, tel. 448-0038, exhibits contemporary art in two galleries. The plaza is at the heart of the new mushrooming downtown, with the **Bonaventure Hotel** at 404 S. Figuerua st. as the centerpiece. The glass, light, winding staircases, transparent elevators and reflecting pools give the structure an other-worldly feel from within. The 34th Lounge (on the 34th floor) offers drinks and a dizzying view.

A new and interesting **Museum of Contemporary Art** is located nearby on 2505 Grand ave., where one can see the development of the arts from the 1940s till today. Open Tues., Wed., Sat., Sun. 11am-6pm. Thurs.-Fri. 11am-8pm. Admission charged. Free Thurs.-Fri. after 5pm, tel. 626-6222.

The **Civic Center** area, bounded by Temple, Main, 1st and Spring streets (with a little spillover across these boundaries), encompasses the largest concentration of government bureaucracy outside Washington D.C. As with other civic centers, the scattered presence of homeless people on the lawns highlights a certain irony.

There was a time when, from the observation deck on the 27th floor of **City Hall**, you could see from the San Gabriel Mountains to the sea; today, you must first check smog conditions, 200 N.Spring st. Open Mon.-Fri. 8am-5pm. Admission free. Free 45-minute tours, Mon.-Fri. 10-11am. Call two days ahead for reservations, tel. 485-4423.

Across the street, the **LA Children 's Museum** encourages kids of all ages to handle and play with exhibits. 310 N. Main st. Mon.-Fri. 11:30am-5pm, Sat.-Sun. 10am-5pm. Admission fee charged, tel. 687-8800. It's an unusual, stimulating place, with displays on the city's ethnic communities, and a children's T.V. station.

Keeping the pulse on the bureaucratic complex is the **L.A. Times** at 202 W. 1st St., tours Mon.-Fri. at 3pm. Children must be 10 or over. Meet the guide at the entrance, tel. 972-5000. It is generally considered one of the top newpapers in the country. The free tour takes you behind the headlines.

**Los Angeles Zoo**, is always a good place for a bit of light relief, especially the new **Adventure Island** featuring the diverse animal population of American Southwest in its natural habitat. For additional information contact the **Greater Los Angeles Zoo Association**, 5333 Zoo dr., tel. 213-664-1100.

The **Armand Hammer Museum of Art and Cultural Center** in Westwood will house a $250 million art collection when it opens. For more information, tel. 213-624-7300 (visitors bureau).

**Little Tokyo** is located mainly between 1st and 3rd Streets, between Main and Alameda on the minibus loop. The thriving Japanese population which was uprooted, humiliated and interned during World War II, returned with energy and vigor to create a new community for themselves. This is a quietly interesting neighborhood with tastes of Japanese culture in little pockets all around. The main center is the **Japanese Village Plaza Mall**, with its stone paths and ponds. The plaza and surrounding streets are lined with restaurants, *sushi* bars and small Japanese specialty products, artwork, and books. The toy stores sell some unusual Japanese gimmicks, including weird wind-up monsters and robots. Restaurant windows display bright models of the cuisine that are tantalizing works of art, and delicious enough to eat. *Sushi* is one such example. It has captured the west coast from Los Angeles to Seattle. It basically consists of raw fish and birds' eggs on little beds of rice at $3 for a few pieces. However unappealing this may at first sound, *sushi* is, in fact, exquisite cuisine. From the precise presentation to the delicate blending and contrasts of taste, it is Japanese through and through: elegant, refined, colorful, yet with something sparse about it.

In a land where the visual presentation of food is as important as its taste and quality, the *sushi* chef is both a visual and a culinary artist. He learns his profession during a long apprenticeship, starting with the most menial tasks in the restaurant. It may be a year before he handles a knife. He learns how to select fresh fish, and even the correct preparation of rice may take him years to perfect.

Rice, far from being simply an accompaniment, is the foundation of *sushi*. It is steamed and tossed in a dressing made of rice vinegar, sugar and salt, while simultaneously being fanned to cool quickly. The kernels must be just the right size and consistency to be shaped into pads.

Look for a *sushi* bar where there is a Japanese clientele. Although some *sushi* bars have tables, sit at the counter so you can watch and talk to the chef. He will take your order directly. Watch him perform his rituals of precise preparation. Since the fish is eaten raw, the slicing is crucial. The Japanese have developed it into a highly formalized art. Particular fish must be sliced in particular ways. Some are cut into regular rectangles, some are cubed, others sliced paper thin.

The rectangular or square pieces of *sushi* are set out carefully to blend with the colors. The reds, yellows, gold, translucent pink, deep green of the seaweed casings, and pure white of the fillet combine to make the plate a work of art.

If you are new to the *sushi* world, ask the chef for some suggestions and advice. Although quantities are not huge, *sushi* is very filling. Try some *saki*, tea or Japanese beer with your meal.

The *New Otani Hotel*, on 120 S. Los Angeles st. between 1st and 2nd, symbolizes the growing connection between the Japanese American community and the developing economy of the Pacific nations. One of a chain, the hotel has both American and Japanese rooms. The two-room Japanese suite overlooking the garden and pool costs a mere $250 per night. If that is a bit too much, enjoy a saki at the bar. The new **Japanese American Cultural and Community Center** offers rotating exhibitions in its gallery.

Tours of Little Tokyo, lasting about an hour and a half, are available through the **Little Tokyo Business Association** by pre-arrangement at 244 S. San Pedro st., 501, tel. 620-0570.

At the edge of Little Tokyo is the **Museum of Neon Art** at 704 Traction ave. Admission charged, tel. 617-1580. There are displays of the history, variations and possibilities of what almost amounts to an American folk art.

Many art galleries in downtown Los Angeles have organized under the umbrella of the **Los Angeles Visual Art** (LAVA) movement. Check with LAVA for a report of exhibits at the various member galleries.

The Chinese community of L.A. dates back to the gold rush days of the 1850s. The local Chinese were greatly abused, and in 1871 19 Chinese were killed in riots in which police participated. Deep prejudice and bigotry continued into the next century, albeit a little less violently. The present **Chinatown**, north of Little Tokyo, was built in the 1930s, when the Chinese community was moved from its home near Union station. The deliberate exaggeration and ornateness was part of a conscious effort to attract tourists.

At the gate to Chinatown is a statue of Sun Yat Sen, father of the Chinese Republic. The Chinese in Los Angeles drilled for and later took an active role in the revolt against the Manchu Dynasty. The Chinese markets and the restaurants are enough to whet anyone's appetite, and there are plenty of moderately priced eateries in the Food Mall.

If you are planning to visit Chinatown in San Francisco you may want to pass up coming here.

The **El Pueblo de Los Angeles State Historical Park**, and Olvera

*Souvenirs from Olvera street*

st. preserve what was the founding site of L.A., as well as a number of historical buildings surrounding it. What is today a sprawling city, started as a village of 44 in 1781, with about half of those being children, while the adults consisted largely of Indians, Blacks and Mulattos. A meagre simple village until the 1850s, it was seized by the newly independent Mexico from Spanish rule in 1822, and then seized in turn by the Americans. During the gold rush days the worst American elements — the ones who could not find a footing in the North or were kicked out by vigilantes, drifted down to L.A. and helped make this one of the wildest towns in the West where murder was a daily event and where, for a while, no one would pick up the sherrif's badge. The railroad connection in 1869 brought in streams of immigrants, and, as a result, the downtown area spread west.

**Olvera Street** today is a carefully ornamented Mexican stageset. For a throbbing Mexican atmosphere and much better and cheaper Mexican food, head south to the Grand Central Market.

Near Olvera st. is the city's train depot, **Union Station**, huge and graceful and beautifully decorated in Spanish style. Today the cavernous hall is empty, but when L.A. became a major shipping point for the Pacific theater during World War II, crowds of servicemen lined up at train platforms and ticket booths or waited in line for a last call to their loved ones.

The once lavish theaters on Broadway were built in the early decades of the century for the booming movie business. South Broadway is now a central avenue for the Hispanic section of downtown, as the store signs and movie marquees show. For a pulse of Mexico which you will not get on Olvera st., join the thousands of people from all over the city who flow through the **Grand Central Market** (317 S. Broadway), hunting and finding bargains. Mounds of nuts, fruits, cheeses, squid, eggs, pigs and poultry line the market. Mexican food is plentiful, delicious and authentic.

Nearby is the **Bradbury Building** at 304 S. Broadway, tel. 489-1893. This famous building is a Los Angeles landmark and a site used in many movies. The exterior is plain, but the inside resembles one of Max Escher's self-perpetuating illusions, flooded by light. The building was designed by George Herbert Wyman, a draftsman with no architectural experience, who accepted the commission only after he received a message from his dead brother, and found the inspiration for his design in a 19th-century utopian novel.

The wholesale markets in lower downtown reveal sights that even most locals miss; you need only wake up at or stay up till four of five in the morning. In the huge **flower market** on Wall street between 7th and 8th sts., fresh flowers are frenetically unloaded and haggled over. The bursts of color and scent are almost hallucinatory in the pre-dawn darkness. Trucks packed with luscious California produce from the San Joaquin and Imperial Valleys roll into the produce market's two locations, off 9th and San Pedro, and along Central avenue between 7th and 8th. Men unload the crates, as they shout in a babble of languages. All-night diners and little Mexican cafes serve the workers mounds of ham and eggs or _huevos rancheros_ and cups of steaming coffee.

**Toward Pasadena**
Northeast of downtown, at Highland Park, the **Southwest Museum** houses some of the finest collections of Indian art and artifacts in the United States. Located at 234 Museum Drive, access off the Pasadena Freeway. Open Tues.-Sat. 11am-5pm, Sun. 1-5pm. Admission charged, tel. 221-2163. Permanent exhibits provide vivid visual narrative of the diverse cultures of the Indians of the Great Plains, the Southwest coast and California. Also included are exhibits of Meso-American and South American pre-Columbian pottery artifacts. The museum offers a year-round schedule of lectures, films, music and theatrical events. Hispanic folk and decorative arts are on show in the adjacent **Casa de Adobe**, 4605 Figueroa st.

Admission free. Same hours at the Southwest Museum, which was constructed by a local adobe craftsman.

## Pasadena

Pasadena is one of the older suburbs that first branched out from Los Angeles. Sitting right at the base of the San Gabriel Mountains, there is excellent access to the winding roads and hiking trails that climb the range. Pasadena is known to most of the country as home of the **Tournament of Roses** parade and the **Rose Bowl**, held each New Year's Day. So popular is the event that people camp out overnight to secure good seats.

Pasadena is the home of several excellent museums. The **Norton Simon Museum of Art** is superb; if you only see one art museum in L.A. this must be it. Located at 411 W. Colorado blvd. Open Thurs.-Sun. noon-6pm. Adults $2, $3 on Sunday, students and seniors 75 cents, children free, tel. 818-449-6840. From Rubens and Rembrandt to Van Gogh and Picasso, all the masters are here and all the major movements represented.

Henry Huntington, early railroad mogul, built a lavish 207-acre estate and filled it with art treasures, rare books, and a stunningly landscaped and variegated botanical garden, which is today the **Huntington Library, Art Gallery and Botanical Gardens**, a cultural landmark at 1151 Oxford rd., San Marino, 911080. Open Tues.-Sun.

1-4:30pm. Admission free. $2 parking. For tickets on Sunday, request ahead by mail, with the date requested and a self-addressed stamped envelope, tel. 818-449-3901. The art gallery is installed in what was the residence, and it places a heavy emphasis on 18th and 19th century paintings. The holdings of the library include a Gutenberg Bible. The garden is overwhelming. There are 12 acres of desert plants alone, plus Japanese and Australian gardens, and the 1,060 varieties of roses of Shakespeare's garden.

The renovated **Old Town** of Pasadena, half a mile east of the museum, is colorful but not very interesting.

## Exposition Park

**Exposition Park**, home of several large museums and public buildings, lies south of downtown, too far to walk. Once an open-air market, the area became a haven for horse racing and saloons. The olympic games of 1932 took place here, until an enterprising judge asserted that it was an appropriate place for a cultural center to be built.

You can't miss the complex of the **California Museum for Science and Industry** at 700 State dr. Open 10am-5pm daily. Free admission, tel. 744-7400. Inside you'll find exhibits on subjects ranging from computer technology, to nutrition, anatomy and natural resources.

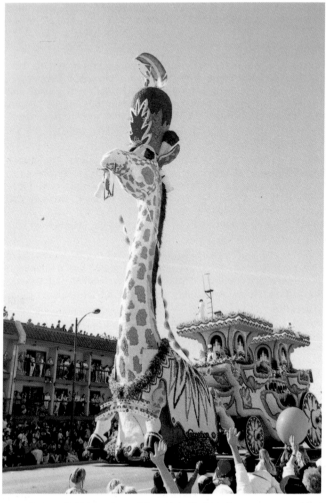

*"Giraffe" at the Tournament of Roses parade, pasadena*

This is a great place to bring children. There are buttons to push and levers to pull everywhere.

Outside the museum is the tranquil and fragrant **Exposition Rose Garden**, with almost 200 varieties of roses. Open daily 10am-5pm. Admission free.

The **California Afro-American Museum** offers an excellent introduction to Black culture, with exhibitions ranging from books clandestinely published by Blacks in the ante-bellum South to contemporary sculpture. 600 State dr. Open daily 10am-5pm. Admission free, tel. 744-7432.

The **County Museum of Natural History** is vast and fantastic, spanning the natural world and development of culture. Located at 900 Exposition blvd. Open Tue-Sun. 10am-5pm. Admission charged, tel. 744-3414 or 744-DINO for tape recorded message.

The huge private **University of Southern California** is famous for such modern disciplines as film and football, but some of the old buildings emanate an aura of medieval scholasticism. The **Fischer Art Gallery**, 823 Exposition blvd., houses the large Armand Hammer collection of 18th and 19th century Dutch paintings. Open Sept.-Apr. noon-5pm. Admission free, tel. 743-2799. For general campus information, tel. 743-2388.

Northeast of USC is the **Hebrew Union College** and its **Skirball Museum**. 3077 University ave. Open Tues.-Fri. 11am-4pm, Sun. 10am-5pm. Admission free, tel. 749-3424. It has a collection of artifacts from Biblical archeology and Judaica from ancient times to present. *A Walk Through Time* recreates a Biblical environment.

The predominantly Black Watts neighborhood boasts the **Watts Towers**, art that is a testimony of persistent imagination and innovation. 1727 E. 107th st. Open Tues.-Fri. 9am-5pm, tel. 569-8181. From 1921 to 1954, working alone, Simon Rodia created towers over 100 ft. (34 m) tall from bedframes, old pipes, scrap metal, and anything else he could find. He scaled the growing towers in a window washer's rig, and decorated them with bits of glass, plates, sea shells and tiles. Rodia eventually moved away, leaving his property to a neighbor. A proposal to have the sculpture demolished sparked a local rescue effort, and it is now a State Historical Park, operated by the city. The **Watts Towers Arts Center** leads tours inside the towers.

## Movie and Television Land

Television studios issue tickets for the viewing of the live taping of their shows. Some are available from the Visitors Information Center in the ARCO plaza. The center will also send them to an in-state address. Out-of-state visitors can receive "guest cards" or a letter by mail which are redeemable for tickets. Inquire at the Visitors' Center.

**Universal Studios** has transformed tours of its back lots into a thriving business in itself. Thousands visit the studios daily. Allow four to six hours for the entire visit, which includes a two-hour tram ride through exhibits of props and scenes followed by the staging of various shows. You will see the house from *Psycho*, stunts from the

*A-Team*. You will be attacked by the shark from *Jaws* and captured by inter-galactic bad guys. But the biggest and newest star on the lot is the gigantic King Kong, who will gaze at you with curiosity as you cross the Brooklyn Bridge, and then roar with rage, so close that you can see his huge cavities and feel his hot banana breath — but don't worry, you will miraculously escape! The best part of the tour is the tram ride. The different shows, however, and the long queues to see them might not appeal to everyone.

Universal is located just off the Hollywood Freeway, via the Barham boulevard or Lankershim boulevard exits. Open 8am-6pm summers and holidays; 10am-3:30pm off-season weekdays, and 9:30am-3:30pm on off-season weekends. Admission is a steep $19.95 from age 12 up; $15.95 ages 3-11. Free under 3; $2 parking. Tel. 818-508-5444.

Not far from Universal, **NBC television studios** offer tours which concentrate less on gimmicks and fanfare, and show more of what the operation of a major commercial studio entails. Visitors are shown some special effects exhibits. You might be chosen to fly across Los Angeles as Superman, or you may meet the stars who happen to be filming that day.

Arrive early to precede the crowds, thereby improving the chances of obtaining free tickets for the live taping of a show, 3000 W. Alameda ave., Burbank, CA, 91523. Tours from 8:30am-4pm weekdays, 10am-4pm Sat., 10am-2pm Sun. Adults $6.50, ages 5-14 $4.50, under 5 free, tel. 818-840-3537. To write for tickets in advance, include the name of the show, the date, number of tickets desired and a self-addressed stamped envelope.

**ABC** offers tickets for show taping. Write ABC-TV, 4151 Prospect, Hollywood 90027. Free television tickets can be obtained from *Audience Unlimited Inc.*, 100 Universal City Plaza, Bldg-153, Universal City, CA, 91608, tel. 818-506-0067.

For tickets to **CBS-TV** shows: *CBS-TV Ticket Office*, 7800 Beverly blvd. Hollywood 90036, Att: Gr 100, tel. 852-2458.

## Hollywood and environs

The corner of **Hollywood and Vine**, once a meeting place and buzzing center of mythic proportions, still best expresses Hollywood today. On one corner is a porno theater, and nearby a store advertising such fashions as sharply studded wristbands. One block away is a tattoo shop. Up Vine is the famous **Capitol Records** headquarters, shaped like a stack of records (one source says it was inspired by Nat King Cole). Down Vine st. is a vegetarian fast-food stand, an Ethiopian restaurant, a blues club and a wig shop with the surrealistic vision of hairdressers preparing wigs on the heads of mannikins in the front window. At night, the streets are patrolled by prostitutes of assorted genders, and preachers of various salvations, as well as punks with hairdos shaped like dinosaur spines, and an occasional wide-eyed youngster lugging his guitar.

In other words, it ain't what it used to be. Stroll down Hollywood Boulevard, but don't expect to see more than a few tawdry, slightly sad, nostalgic remnants of a world so glittery, fantastic and unreal that it could never last.

The area of Hollywood was once a camping ground for the Cahuenga Indians, who were then a small farming community, until some enterprising practitioners of the new fangled technology of motion pictures set up shop in an abandoned tavern. The area attracted more of the same, partly because laws involving the movies were hard to enforce out in these parts, and because Mexico was a hop away. By about 1915, the movie industry was already entrenched and fortunes were being made by producers and stars. Movies provided the narcotic of fantasy during the Depression and the Hollywood studios rolled out hundreds of them. Their creators and stars became fabulously wealthy and created their exclusive colonies in Beverly Hills, Belle Aire and Malibu Canyon. Gaudy neo-classical architecture sprang up in private mansions, department stores and theaters themselves.

Hollywood's dominance did not last as most of the studios moved over the hills. The huge giants were challenged by smaller independent studios. Stars grew more independent and assertive in creating their roles (and their box office percentage). Television, too, helped speed the studios' demise.

On **Hollywood Boulevard** you can still see glimpses of the glitter that pervaded. Just look at the sidewalk, where the names of numerous stars are enshrined.

Hollywood's most famous symbol is **Graumann's Chinese Theater**, a strange collection of pagoda like entrances, dragons' faces and tails. The same Sid Graumann erected his **Egyptian Theater** (6708 Hollywood blvd.), where the usherettes were outfitted like Cleopatra.

The **Chinese Theater**, 6925 Hollywood blvd., tel. 464-8111, opened in 1927 with the premiere of Cecil B. De Mille's *King of Kings*. Afterwards it became famous for its shots of stars exiting from limousines and strolling into the theater past crowds of ogling and drooling fans. Graumann himself wrote and directed shows to introduce the movies, some bordering on the outrageous. He cemented the fame of his stars with imprints of various appendages in wet cement in the theater courtyard. Today, every tourist wanders around the courtyard staring at the signatures. Alas, Graumann's theater is no longer Graumann's, as it was bought up by the Mann theater chain, and is now officially called Mann's Chinese Theater. Movies are still shown there.

Near the Chinese Theater are numerous tour companies offering

*Capitol Records headquarters — shaped like a stack of records*

*Chinese Theater*

guided tours of the stars' homes in Beverly hills. If you want to take the tour by car, you can buy a map here. They are also sometimes sold on various corners near the Beverly Hills area, but you are more assured of obtaining one on Hollywood blvd. The tour guides on the buses, though corny and sometimes obviously bored, can at least tell some juicy stories you wouldn't get driving along a winding road, messing with a map and trying to squint through the foliage at Charlie Chaplin's house. So, as long as you're playing the gawking tourist, you might as well pay about $10 and get your money's worth.

**Hollywood on Location** provides the chance to see live stars at work, 8644 Wilshire. About $20 for the service, tel. 659-9165. Every morning this office publishes a list of shooting locations with directions, maps, stars, the shot, etc. You'll need a car for a day to make full use of the information.

The **Capitol Records Tower** conducts free tours on Tuesdays and Thursdays, 1756 Vine, tel. 462-6252. **On Location**, installed in a refurbished drug store, features several scale models of old Hollywood, built with exactness and detail, and accompanied by miniature spotlights and dramatic music and narration. For all the kitsch, it gives a good feel for Hollywood in its heyday. In contrast to this, the Hollywood Wax Museum is not really worthwhile.

The decaying heart of movieland has an excellent concentration of bookstores, once haunted by the writers attracted to Hollywood by high and regular script fees. The selections are wide and varied, and are a goldmine for anyone interested in movie history. At the corner of Hollywood boulevard and Las Palmas is a long newsstand stacked with periodicals from around the country and the world. The boulevard has a number of inexpensive ethnic foodstands serving satisfying portions of Italian, Middle Eastern, Mexican and Chinese cuisine. Its costume shops will outfit you with a jewelled crown, giant sword and horrifying mask for your next soiree. Perhaps some sociological insights can be gleaned from **The International Love Boutique**, toward the west end of the boulevard's commercial strip. Ten years ago, its jokes, props and rubber gadgets would have been sold behind a door marked XXX, but today they are displayed in a chic scented setting with soft music.

The **Hollywood Bowl**, 2301 N. Highland ave., tel. 213-876-8742, designed by Frank Lloyd Wright, is a delightful place for a concert on a summer evening. Tradition calls for a picnic beforehand. The wooden seats are hard, so its worth bringing a pillow. Some seats allow a view of the huge HOLLYWOOD sign, which makes you feel — well, in Hollywood. The **Los Angeles Philharmonic** regularly plays "the bowl", as do star performers from all realms of world music. Students and seniors with identification are eligible for $5 tickets to any Tuesday or Thursday L.A. Philharmonic concerts, as well as some others performed by the orchestra. These "rush" tickets are on sale the day before and on the day of a concert at the Hollywood Bowl box office. The evenings can be cool, so bring a sweater. There is a mid-priced restaurant on the grounds selling pre-packaged dinners. Concerts can get crowded and parking difficult. Call for details on special park-and-ride buses to the amphitheater from various locations throughout the L.A. area. The amphitheater is accessible to the handicapped, and a brochure titled *Guide to the Hollywood Bowl for Patrons with Disabilities* is available upon request by phone, tel. 876-8742.

**The Museum on the Development of Music in Los Angeles** is small but very interesting, giving a glimpse of the popularization of jazz and blues, 2301 N. Highland ave. Take the Highland ave. exit from the Hollywood Freeway, tel. 876-8742.

The famous **Hollywood Sign**, erected in 1923, hovering over Mt. Cahuenga above the Hollywood Freeway, was originally part of an advertisement for a subdivision called Hollywoodland. Acquired by the local Chamber of Commerce, the sign was refurbished and edited into a larger than life advertisement and symbol.

Toward the east end of Hollywood, north of downtown, Silver Lake and Echo Park give Hollywood more of a neighborhood feeling. The **Street Fair** at Sunset and Santa Monica boulevards held in August, attracts a wild mixture of characters.

## The Sunset Strip

**Sunset Boulevard**, the traditional center of West Hollywood, was once the hub of nightlife in the city. After a hard day's work at the studio, it was natural for the star being chauffeured home to Beverly Hills, Brentwood or Malibu to stop at one of the posh clubs on Sunset. In the 1960s, Sunset became the magnet for psychedelics and flower children. Then, when the flower children began to wilt, Sunset attracted more hard-core weirdos per square foot than any other street in the city or state. Today it has renewed its place as a bejeweled string of chic night spots, mostly rock clubs.

Looking south from various points along Sunset at night, the vast glimmering grid of Los Angeles is visible and overwhelming as is the array of huge handpainted billboards. Do not think that only stars make it up there. Rich hopefuls have been known to attract attention for their clients from the many producers who drive this way to their homes in the western hills. Several comedy clubs have appeared here, presenting famous comedians and those longing to become one. On amateur nights the admission is usually cheaper, but then you must take your chances; you might glimpse tomorrow's Woody Allen, but you might squirm in embarrassment for the poor performer all night long.

The Fairfax area, squeezed in near West Hollywood and Beverly Hills, has an ambience of its own, considerably more modest than its neighbors. The main sights are the Farmer's Market, the CBS studios and the Jewish section.

The **Farmer's Market**, at the corner of Third street and Fairfax, is a puffed up tourist rip-off. Not in every farmer's market can you buy a replica of a classical vase or a David Bowie poster. It was once a real farmer's market selling real produce at reasonable or even cheap prices. Although the produce can still be found, and though it often looks beautiful, reasonable bargains are rare. The food bars, however, sell an amazing array of cuisine and delicacies. Top off your crepe or shrimp salad with Chinese chestnuts or toffee peanuts.

Near the Farmer's Market are the **CBS Television Studios** where various game shows are broadcast before live audiences. Tickets must be arranged in advance, tel. 852-2624.

Just two blocks up begins the concentrated **Jewish section** of Fairfax. A center for the Jewish community since World War II, Fairfax still has an Eastern European atmosphere, though many families have left. More than a pinch of the Middle East has been added now that immigrants from Israel have begun to congregate here. On the street you will hear Hebrew, some Yiddish, and a little English. Bakeries, kosher delis, Israeli restaurants and *felafel* stands line the street. A potato knish or two can keep you going a long while.

Several stores specialize in Jewish books and Jewish and Israeli music. A large newsstand at Fairfax and Oakwood carries international periodicals. A few semi open-air markets sell produce far more cheaply than the Farmer's Market down the street. With other small ethnic restaurants moving in — Korean and Yugoslavian, for example — the street has the atmosphere of a city neighborhood not found much in L.A. these days.

## Griffith Park

In the hills northeast of Hollywood is **Griffith Park**. With 4,000 acres, it is the largest municipal park in the country. A large portion was left undeveloped for hiking and riding. Maps are available at the four main park entrances. Bus 97 goes to the park, but it is hard to get around here without a car.

The **Greek Theater** is a beautiful place for an evening concert, and there are presentations of everything from classical music to Neil Diamond, tel. 216-6666. Nearby is the cool, shaded **bird sanctuary**, which is as much a sanctuary for people. Walking tours are given on Sunday at 1pm. Open daily from dawn to dusk. Children can ride the railroad and climb on trolleys, old cars, planes and ponies at **Travel Town**, 200 drive, tel. 662-5874. The distinguished white building with the green copper dome is the **Griffith Observatory and Planetarium**, a L.A. landmark. The Hall of Science offers basic displays with lots of button-pushing. The planetarium show is done well, and the popular Laserium will bombard you with sound and light. There is a telescope for public use on summer evenings until 10pm and in winter from Tues.-Sun. 7-10pm. Admission charged.

Planetarium shows: Open daily during summer, 1:30pm, 3pm and 8pm, Sat.-Sun. also 4:30pm. In winters Tues.-Fri. at 3pm and 8pm, Sat.-Sun. 4:30pm. Admission, seniors discount, tel. 664-1181 or

664-1191 for tape-recorded message. For Laserium schedule and programs, tel. 818-997-3624.

The **Los Angeles Zoo**, though not on the level of the San Diego Zoo, is interesting, with animals grouped by continent. Many touchable creatures for children, 5333 Zoo dr. Open 10am-6pm in summer, 10am-5pm in winter. Admission charged, tel. 666-4090.

There are over 40 miles (64 km) of horse trails in the park and commercial stables on the park's edges. They only take cash and require a deposit.

A great network of hiking trails picks up from various points in the park. The bird sanctuary and observatory trails lead to the top of Mt. Hollywood from where you can see all of the L.A. basin. Several guided hikes begin at the ranger station on Crystal Spring rd. Free trail maps are available here, tel. 665-5188.

## Wishire/Hancock Park

During the real estate boom of the 1880s, an entrepreneur named H. Gaylord Wilshire portioned out a tract along a country lane and named it after himself. After Edward Doheny discovered oil, wells popped up all through the neighborhood and property values shot higher than the black geysers.

A line of stores built during the 1930s was dubbed the **Miracle Mile** to attract shoppers from the central city. This section has some of the finest examples of the old art deco architecture that proliferated in Los Angeles. The gem of the street, **Bullocks Wilshire** was touted as the city's first suburban store. Set up as an elegant establishment to draw the wealthy from downtown, it retains that image today, including its 5th-floor tea room.

**Wilshire blvd**. extends for 16 miles (25 km) from downtown to the Pacific, cutting through the financial district, through neighborhoods of Asian and Latin American immigrants, through the old stylish neighborhood of Hancock Park, through Miracle Mile, and finally out to trendy Santa Monica.

The strangest sight along gleaming Wilshire is the ancient mastodon wallowing through a pond of black tar in the **La Brea Tar Pits**. You can almost hear it bellowing in fear and frustration. In 1910 the first fossil discoveries were made at the La Brea pits, which ultimately yielded the well-preserved remains of an enormous variety of animal life from the Pleictocene period, down to about 6000 BC. Mastodons, saber-tooth tigers, ground sloths and native American horses, all roamed the area now covered by housing tracts and parking lots. Among the other remains were those of a woman.

**The George C. Page Museum** displays the findings from the adjacent tar pits, 5801 Wilshire blvd. Open Tue.-Sun. 10am-5pm. Admission charged. Free on the second Tuesday of each month. For a recorded message call Tel. 936-2230, for other queries call Tel. 857-6311. Through a variety of techniques, bones have been fleshed out, thereby recreating a vivid picture of the area's natural history and the evolution of the animals. Through plate-glass windows visitors can observe paleontologists at work. This museum is imaginative and thought-provoking.

The **Los Angeles County Museum of Art**, 5905 Wilshire blvd. Open Tues.-Fri. 10am-5pm, Sat.-Sun. 10am-6pm, tel. 857-6000. Immediately west of the tar pits and Page Museum, the museum consists of three separate buildings which house some amazing collections from all regions and all historical periods of the world: ancient Near Eastern, Western European painting and sculpture, American Painting. The collection of Indian, Tibetan and Nepalese art is highly acclaimed. A sculpture garden featuring bronzes by Rodin connects the buildings. On Monday evenings in winter there are concerts of contemporary music. On weekends the museum's plaza turns bright and lively with street performers. There is a cafeteria, museum shop and art rental gallery. Guided tours of the permanent collections are available.

The **Craft and Folk Art Museum** across Wilshire, is a small museum featuring both the traditional and contemporary in folk art, 5814 Wilshire blvd. Open Tues.-Sun. 11am-5pm, admission charged, tel. 937-5544. The balcony of the *Egg and the Eye* restaurant peers out over the exhibition floor.

South of the towers and elegant stores of Wilshire, in a nondescript, predominantly Black neighborhood of small houses and bungalows, there is a surprisingly rich collection of art in the museums and galleries. **St. Elmo Village**, 4830 St. Elmo dr., tel. 931-3409, is a non-profit community arts center, surrounded by gardens, sculptures and color. On the sidewalk, in the courtyard, on fences and garage doors there are beautiful and blazing murals.

The creation of the village began when the land was slated to be sold. Two artists who had lived there initiated what became a huge grassroots effort to buy the property and turn it into a neighborhood center. Funds were raised with snowballing support from neighbors, community groups, politicians and celebrities. Now, in a neighborhood of gangs and easy access to drugs, the village fosters creativity, community pride and constructive achievement. The artists who live in the village offer workshops to children, the elderly and anyone interested. On Sunday a small cafe is open, with photos on the wall relating the birth and history of the center. The annual **Festival of the Art of Survival** initiated as a fund-raiser, has become a jam-packed colorful celebration, often attended by prominent local leaders, such as Mayor Tom Bradley and big-name performers. The village welcomes visitors, 4830 St. Elmo dr., tel. 931-3409.

Further along Wilshire, art of a different sort can be found at the **Martyrs Memorial and Museum of the Holocaust**, in the Jewish Community Building, 6505 Wilshire blvd. Open Mon.-Thurs. 9am-5pm, Fri. 9am-3pm, Sun. 1-5pm. Admission free, tel. 852-1234 ext 3200. The museum presents a stark presentation of Hitler's "final solution." The presentations can shock, but the paintings and drawings created by people trapped in ghettos and death camps are amazing and inspiring statements.

## Beverly Hills

At the turn of the century, the Beverly Hills region was open rolling farmland where shepherds grazed their flocks. Some oil speculators, hoping to cash in on the region's oil boom, purchased the property, but the wells turned no profit. The investors, to recover their losses, sub-divided the property for an exclusive subdivision, near but separate from the growing city of Los Angeles. By 1914, the wealthy had bought tracts and were moving in. Douglas Fairbanks started the migration of movie stars to the area. He bought land and developed it into Picfair, his private residence at 1143 Summit dr. where he lived with Mary Pickford. Separate municipal status allowed the stars and wealthy to develop their enclave as they wished, which meant no annoying industry and strict regulations on parking, signs and preservation of trees.

The main shopping area is formed by the triangle of Wilshire blvd., Little Santa Monica blvd. (a smaller street just to the south of and parallel to Santa Monica blvd.), and **Rodeo Drive**. Rodeo drive is famous for its exclusive stores: Gucci, Ralph Lauren, Yves St. Tropez, and many more. The *Beverly Wilshire Hotel*, considered one of the most prestigious in the world, is an enormous spread out structure with cobblestones and marble arches. The oasis of accessibility within this opulence is the Foodshow.

At the southwest corner of Beverly Hills is **Century City**, a complex of condos and an even more expensive shopping area extending over a three-block long strip between Santa Monica blvd. and Pico along the Avenue of the Stars. This was the 20th Century-Fox back lot until the studio found it more economical to shoot on location. The **ABC Entertainment Center** is found here (see "Movie and Television Land"). Also in the complex is **The Hollywood Experience**, a multi-screen one-hour show on the history of tinseltown, tel. 553-0626.

Some of the city's most famous, elaborate and expensive restaurants are found on **Restaurant Row**, La Cienega blvd. between San Vincente and Wilshire. Famous among the famous is *Lawry's Prime Rib*.

In stark contrast to the ornamentation of Century City, is the adjacent **Simon Weisenthal Center**, the comprehensive museum and archives on the Holocaust and related contemporary human rights issues, 9760 W. Pico blvd. Open Mon.-Thurs. 10:30am-4:30pm, Fri. 10:30am-2:30pm, Sun. 11am-4pm. Admission free, tel. 553-9036. The museum includes original memorabilia and publications. The center offers a steady schedule of lectures, films and educational programs on the Holocaust

The most amazing homes in Beverly Hills are, predictably, in the hills. Some can barely be seen from the road. Buy yourself a star-gazing map if you wish from the vendors along Sunset blvd. or from the souvenir shops along Hollywood blvd. Guided tours are also available. (See 'Hollywood and Environs'.)

The *Beverly Hills Hotel*, near the corner of Sunset and Benedict Canyon rd., is a four-story luxurious example of mission architecture, set back amid 12 acres of lush grounds. It was built in 1912, with many subsequent replacements and additions. Film stars often relax at the hotel's *Polo Lounge*.

**Greystone Park** was built by Edward L. Doheny, years after he had, as a laborer, discovered oil with his shovel and was smart enough to exploit his finding. His baronial mansion overlooking Los Angeles symbolizes an amazing story of one man's rise to wealth and power. The stables, tennis courts, kennels and lake paved over for parking, and the 55-room mansion are all testament to the vastness of his wealth. The main building is closed to the public, but the grounds are open and summer concerts are held here, 905 Loma Vista dr. Open 10am-5pm. Admission free. For ticket information and tour reservations, tel. 550-4796.


## Westwood Village, UCLA

Westwood Village was a small Mediterranean style shopping center until the **University of California at Los Angeles (UCLA)** opened to the north of it. Westwood now serves a huge student body. The nice thing about this area is that there is much to do in an area small enough to walk through — no car is needed. There are campus museums, beautiful buildings and gardens, and a steady schedule of activities.

Westwood is filled with restaurants and theaters. First-run movies are shown at a hefty $6 per ticket. The shops and galleries are bizarre, exotic and chic. On weekend nights the scene is manic, as youths, punks, performers, and tourists join the trim, tanned students who pour out of the campus area.

The main street, **Westwood Boulevard**, runs south from the campus to Wilshire. The intersection is insanely busy. Some of the more interesting shops and restaurants are on the side streets. The smaller and more unusual bookstores are clustered on Westwood blvd. south of Wilshire. Car traffic through campus is limited, and parking is tough. Buses 20, 21 or 308 run along Wilshire to Westwood. From the parking lot 32 on Weyburn st. there is a free shuttle to campus.

You can sometimes find parking spots south of Wilshire or on the hilly streets south of campus where the fraternities are. It may be better to accept fate, drive into one of the university parking lots and pay $3 for the day. The RTD Westwood shuttle runs from 6:30pm to 1am on Friday, and 11am-1:30am on Saturday. Route maps are available at various spots in Westwood or in a *RTD* customer service center. The shuttle runs to the Federal Building at Veteran and Ashton, just south of Wilshire, where there is free parking.

UCLA is rated one of the top universities in the country. The school is well-known for its graduate programs, perhaps its medical school in particular. The campus is beautifully landscaped and it is easy and tempting to get lost here. **The Quadrangle** near the center of the campus was featured in the film *The Graduate* as the campus of Berkeley (other scenes were shot in Berkeley). The visitor center is in the **Ueberroth Building** on Leconte ave. Tours and maps are available here. Open Mon.-Fri. 8am-5pm, tel. 825-4338.

**Ackerman Union** is the student center. Many films are offered on campus but rules forbid their announcement off-campus. At the Union (as well as bulletin boards around campus) you can catch up on everything. This is the buzzing central hive of all student activity. Downstairs there is travel information, a ride board, a bowling alley, cafeteria, and smaller eateries reasonably priced for student budgets, tel. 825-0611.

The **Murphy Sculpture Garden** exhibits pieces by Rodin, Lipschitz and Moore, among others. The **Museum of Cultural History**, at the southern part of the campus has exhibits of folk and primitive art. The observation deck of the **Ralph Bunche Social Work Building** affords a view of the campus, hills, coast and ocean on a clear day. Near the Quad is **Royce Hall**, named for noted Californian historian Josiah Royce. Recently refurbished, its auditorium hosts top performers. For ticket information, tel. 825-2953. The **Mathias Botanical Garden**, in the corner of the campus, is a shaded area of redwoods and palms, a beautiful place for a picnic or just to rest in a peaceful and shady spot.

## Around Malibu

From L.A. County's northern border with Ventura County, its coast is dotted with state beaches and parks. The beaches may be narrow and rocky, or broad and smooth. Some are backed by cliffs, while others slope gently.

On a hot summer's day it seems that half the basin's population flocks to the L.A. beaches, but despite crowded roads, parking problems and crowds, there is always room on the beach. Even on a crowded beach you are spared that east-coast phenomenon of picking your way over oil-covered bodies and spreading your blanket as if staking a gold claim.

**Leo Carillo State Beach**, in the north, is a favorite for windsurfers. Across the road is the outlet for a network of trails penetrating into the valleys, canyons and chaparral-covered hills, tel. 818-706-1310. Several beaches to the south is **Zuma Beach**, which is county-owned. It is comparatively large, with concessions, restrooms and crowds. To the south juts **Duma Point**, and on the other side of it is a beautiful crescent shaped beach, hidden by tall bluffs. This is a hot spot for surfers and their groupies. Duma Point gives a view of the coast in both directions, and clearly shows where the beach was washed away in the giant storms of 1983. Guns were positioned here during World War II against the Japanese invasion that never came. Be careful parking; local authorities regularly hunt down illegally parked cars and slap on hefty fines.

The stretch of beach at Malibu was once owned by the Rindge family, who did their best to keep it private and intact. When the husband died his widow fought the authorities with everything from lawsuits to dynamite, but public transportation and private developers won out. Jutting far west beyond Los Angeles, **Malibu** has its own special atmosphere, and stunning beaches where the scrubby mountains slope down to the sea. It rapidly became a haunt for Hollywood stars. Rock stars from the Beach Boys to Joni Mitchell and Bob Dylan have immortalized Malibu. This is where the beauties come, where the muscles flex, where beaches are private and where the sheriff wears bright green shorts and matching T-shirt. Along this stretch of beach are intermittent public beaches, some with facilities. Roadside stands are interspersed with expensive seafood restaurants perched above the waves. Just east of town are several popular beaches. Parking is expensive. Cars park on the Pacific Coast Highway while there's room.

The **Paul J. Getty Museum**, off the Pacific Coast Highway in Malibu, offers a taste of culture that seems incongruous with the sun worshippers just across the street. An enormous recreation of a Roman country house, the museum displays a magnificent private collection of Western art. It is mind-boggling to see how much great art one man could acquire. Getty devoted himself to preserving these treasures for posterity and public appreciation. He lived most of his life in Europe and, ironically, never saw the museum he created.

The Getty collection emphasizes five major areas: Greek and Roman antiquities, 18th century decorative art (clocks, chairs, carpets, etc.), Western European paintings from the 13th to the 19th century, drawings of the old masters, and illuminated medieval and Renaissance manuscripts. The museum also runs a library, mostly for the work of researchers and scholars. All galleries and most gardens are accessible by wheelchair. Lectures on art are held every Thursday evening. The museum also has a tea room and bookstore.

Parking facilities are limited, and advance parking reservations are required, preferably at least a week in advance. Visitors without a car, or who are unable to make parking reservations, may enter the museum grounds by bicycle, motorcycle, taxi or *RTD* bus 434 (request a museum pass from the bus driver). Located at 17985 Pacific Coast Highway, one mile southeast of Topanga Canyon rd. Open Tues.-Sun 10am-5pm. Gate closes at 4:30pm. Parking, admission and lectures are free. For parking reservations and lecture reservations, tel. 458-2003.

From the Pacific Coast Highway, a turn onto **Topanga Canyon blvd.** leads into the rugged Santa Monica Mountains. This island of wilderness is right in the middle of the metropolis, squeezed between the San Fernando Valley suburbs on the north, Santa Monica and the rest of L.A. on the south, the Ventura Freeway on the east and the ocean on the west. Within these boundaries is a maze of winding roads with hairpin turns. Wend your way with a map north and west to **Malibu Canyon rd.** for spectacular views of the hill, canyon; coastline and ocean. Altenatively, you can follow Mulholland dr. and Mulholland Highway along the crest of the mountains.

**Topanga Canyon** once sheltered opium dealers, smugglers, rum-runners and a brothel. Ensconsced here today are the hippest of the rich and richest of the hip. This is commune, ashram and religious-retreat country. The town of Topanga Canyon, with its organic restaurants and cafes, preceded, and outlasted the hippie movement.

The Santa Monica Mountains provide beautiful hiking trails ranging from easy to rugged. **Malibu Creek State Park**, accessible either by Malibu Canyon rd. from the Pacific Coast Highway, or from the south on Las Virgenes from the Ventura Freeway, is a secluded park with a creek, a lake and 15 miles (25 km) of trails. Bicycling and riding available, no camping, 28754 Mulholland dr., tel. (818) 706-1310.

The larger Topanga State Park also has beautiful trails for hikers and riders, tel. (818) 706-1310. From Topanga Canyon rd., turn west on Entrada rd.

## Santa Monica

South of the hilly peninsula jutting into the ocean at Malibu, nestles Santa Monica and Santa Monica Bay. About 15 miles (25 km) west of downtown and connected by the Santa Monica Freeway, Santa Monica was once a resort village for city residents. Today, its beaches and bluffs are popular and its pier with its amusements has become a landmark. But Santa Monica still clings to a certain apartness. Incorporated as its own city, it is a center for liberal and socialist activism. Liberal forces have gained substantial representation (Tom Hayden, one of the radical student leaders of the 1960s, who married Jane Fonda, is the state assemblyman from Santa Monica). Interests urging greater development have met stiff organized resistance from groups urging strict controls on growth. The rent control laws (often viewed as radical, leftist or progressive legislation) are extremely stringent here in protecting tenants.

The deceptively pretty bay actually hides a serious problem. For more than 20 years, industries discharged huge amounts of DDT and other toxins into the ocean off Santa Monica. The kelp beds, mussels, fish and invertebrates that thrived in these waters have declined and some have disappeared.

Despite recent steps to prevent further dumping and to clean up the bay, the concentrations of DDT found in fish in Santa Monica Bay are reportedly among the highest in the world.

It is easy to understand why the city is popular with young professionals and singles, and the artists who managed to slip in before rents lept up. One could stay in Santa Monica and have all major needs satisfied. The beach and pier, the trendy shops, the downtown shopping center and the bluff park are in close proximity. The bluff park is filled with joggers, walkers, chess-players, and some homeless types who stretch their sleeping bags beneath the wind-sculpted trees. The beaches below are wide, roomy even on a crowded weekend. The famous **Santa Monica Pier**, battered and partly washed out during heavy 1983 storms, is still a popular place to stroll. Hints of yesterday are found in the old boardwalk, the painted signs and hand-carved horses on the carousel, which was seen in the movie *The Sting*.

The Pacific Coast Highway comes down from the north and turns inland at Santa Monica. From the east, the Santa Monica Freeway provides the easiest access. Streets and the beach to the south run into Venice. Parking near the beach area is difficult. But there is cheap and sufficient municipal parking a few blocks inland off Santa Monica blvd. For a couple of bucks you park almost all day.

Santa Monica runs its own bus company. The express bus 10 runs to downtown Los Angeles. If you want to reach downtown Los Angeles, parking your car in the Santa Monica municipal lot and riding the express bus 10 is highly recommended. It takes about 45 minutes (the route along city streets can take twice that). Two buses also run to Venice.

Bicycling is a convenient and popular way to travel along the stretch of beach. A bicycle path starts at Santa Monica and heads south through Venice to Marina Del Ray. To the north, cyclists follow the Pacific Coast Highway.

Touring and bus information is available at the **Visitors Assistance Stand** in Ocean ave. near Arizona st. Open daily 10am-4pm in summer; Tues.-Sun. 11am-3pm in winter, tel. 393-7593.

Santa Monica's older, outside shopping mall, along 2nd and 4th sts.

*Musician at Venice Beach*

between Broadway and Colorado, has some small and interesting shops and no traffic. But this has been appended to the modern **Santa Monica Place**, a slick and trendy version of other indoor malls.

Further south, on Main st. between Ocean Park and Pico, are two blocks of restaurants, boutiques, galleries, antique and specialty shops. Most are geared toward the young upwardly mobile or already-arrived. Here you'll find some small bars where the locals hang out.

If you wish to have a Victorian-style feeling, visit the **Santa Monica Heritage Museum** on 2612 Main st. Open Thurs.-Sun. noon-4pm, tel. 392-8537. The building is more interesting than the different galleries and collections.

Santa Monica, with its hip population and concentration of neighborhoods with small houses, is excellent turf for a favorite southern Californian past-time: 'yard-saling'. People cruise around the neighborhood in their cars at weekends, following the cardboard signs tacked to telephone poles that will lead them to the numerous yard-sales and, hopefully, fantastic bargains. With a little hunting they can be found.

## Venice

The Hare Krishna are out dancing, chanting and jingling tambourines. The one-man electric band on roller skates weaves among the muscled strutters, the gawking tourists, the punks, joggers, jugglers and black kids dancing. The outdoor cafes are packed. Middle Eastern music blares from a booth selling cassettes. A greying man stands on a bench attacking the government while from another bench a preacher in a green irridescent suit proffers God with the slick rhythm of a huckster selling miracle serum... It's a typical summer Sunday on **Venice Beach.**

The American version of Venice was founded in 1904 by tobacco magnate Abbot Kinney, who came west hoping to help the Indians, but succumbed instead to a fantastic vision. Kinney became determined to single-handedly create a mecca for high culture in America, and to recreate an imitation of Venice, Italy. He dug 30 miles of canals, imported gondolas and gondoliers, and created replicas of Italian palazzos and arcades. For a while, the rich of Los Angeles flocked to the pleasures and posh clubs of Venice, but gradually the place deteriorated physically, and then socially. Venice became a tawdry, seedy carnival which attracted hustlers and eccentrics, as well as artists, outcasts and radicals. By 1930 the area had been absorbed by the city and all but a few miles of the canals had been filled.

The old run-down buildings offered comparatively cheap rents, attracting artists and social rebels, outcasts and hard-timers. During the 1950s Venice became L.A.'s outpost for the Beatniks, during the 1960s for the hippies, and during the 1970s for casualties and survivors of both previous epochs.

Almost invisible beneath the glittering eccentricity of Venice lives another group of survivors, the old Eastern European Jews.

Once 10,000 strong, with thriving cultural and social centers, this community has steadily diminished through the pressures of urban development that pushed them out and the natural ravages of time. Some sit on benches, facing the ocean or the parade of humanity. They play backgammon or chess, and read the Yiddish papers. Some, old radicals from another world, pass out political pamphlets to young people.

Venice is easily accessible from Santa Monica by bus, automobile or bicycle or on foot. Pacific Ocean Park, marking the northern end of the beach walk, has a sizable parking lot. Parking along the streets near the beach, especially during the summer, can be a trying exercise in patience, but parking can be found some blocks to the east.

A tour of Venice simply involves walking and taking in the crowds. At Winwood and Pacific, a few blocks in from the beach, are the last vestiges of the colonnaded arcade which was part of Kinney's creation. Windwood and Main, where the streets form a traffic circle, was once a circular canal that formed the hub of the system. The post office on the west side contains a mural illustrating the history of Venice. Between Venice and Washington blvds., just east of the ocean front walk, lies one of the last segments of the canal, filled with ducks, lined with little bungalows and crossed by arched bridges. Watch for the beautiful murals along the boardwalk area. There are several huge and detailed depictions of Venice, such as Venice under a blanket of snow. At the southern end of Ocean Walk, at Washington, is the pier with its bars and restaurants, and beyond that begins opulent Marina Del Ray. Some of the ocean side cafes and restaurants stay open late, but in general the area empties quickly and closes down with sundown. Street people fill the doorways, only to be moved along by the cops. This can be a dangerous area at night.

## Important addresses and phone numbers

Greater Los Angeles Visitors and Convention Bureau: 515 S. Flower st. 90071 (in ARCO plaza), tel. 689-8822. (see "Orientation".)
*Welcome to Los Angeles*: tel. 628-5857. 24-hour recording on current and special events.
Beverly Hills Visitor Bureau: 239 S. Beverly dr., 90212, tel. 271-8174.
Burbank (Greater) Visitor and Convention Bureau: 425-A S. Victory blvd., Burbank 91502, tel. 818-845-4266. Information on some of the studios that moved out this way.
Marina del Rey Chamber: 4629-A Admiralty Way 90292, tel. 821-0555, gives details on the marina's many hotels.
Summer Festival: tel. 876-8742, gives details on an annual festival filled with music celebrities.
Immigration Office: Federal Building, 300, N. Los Angeles st. For extension of a tourist visa.

National Park Service: 22900 Ventura blvd., Woodland Hills, tel. 818-888-3770; For information on the Park Service lands in the Santa Monica Mountains.

Mexican Government Tourism Office: 10100 Santa Monica blvd. suite 224, LA 90067, tel. 203-8151; General information and brochures for visits to Mexico.

Post Office: If you wish to get mail it should be mailed for the General Delivery, 901 S. Broadway, 90055, tel. 617-4413.

Beach and Surf Reports: tel 457-9701.

Highway Conditions: tel. 626-7231.

Weather: tel. 554-1212.

*Ticketron*: 6060 W. Manchester ave., tel. 216-6666.

**Emergency:**
Emergency: tel. 911.

Rape Crisis Hotline: tel. 855-3506.

Legal Aid Hotlines: tel. 487-3320.

Hospital: Cedars - Sinai Medical Center, 8700 Beverly blvd., tel. 855-6517.

Free Clinic: tel. 818-763-8836.

# Around Los Angeles

## Long Beach and Palos Verdes

The rocky **Palos Verdes Peninsula** forms an almost right-angled buttress separating Santa Monica Bay from the south-facing harbors of San Pedro and Long Beach. The **Palos Verdes drive** follows the contours of this outcropping and is lined with exclusive homes. Much of the beach is private. The public beaches are not easily accessible, but for those willing to scramble down to them, they can offer a solitude rarely found along L.A.'s coast.

The **Long Beach Airport** serves major national carriers and is accessible from most major cities. Like LAX, it operates commuter flights to San Francisco, yet is spared the jams and delays endemic to LAX. It is a small, single-terminal airport, and passengers can be in or out in 15 minutes. Nearby are hotels, public transportation and car rentals. Within 15 minutes you can reach a motel near a quiet beach. Forty-five minutes by freeway brings you into downtown L.A., about the same time or less than it would take after waiting for luggage and fighting crowds and traffic around LAX. Forty-five minutes south and you are cruising through little beach towns.

The **Wayfarer's Chapel**, was built in 1949 by Lloyd Wright, son of Frank Lloyd Wright, 5755 Palos Verdes dr. S., Rancho Palos Verdes. Open 10am-4pm, tel. 377-1650. It is a stunning glass church surrounded by redwoods. Built to honor Emanuel Swedenborg, the philospher/theologian, it is used for many weddings today.

The lush 87 acres of the **South Coast Botanic Gardens** are a popular local site, 26300 Crenshaw blvd., Rancho Palos Verdes. Open daily 9am-5pm. Admission charged, tel. 377-0468.

**Marineland** is part-aquarium, part-amusement park, with trained dolphins and killer whales that perform tricks and splash the audience on command, 6600 Palos Verdes dr. S., Palos Verdes. Open Wed.-Sun. 10am-7pm. Adults $9.95, ages 3-11 $6.95, seniors $5. During winter, check to confirm hours, tel. 541-5663. For an extra fee, visitors can swim in a tank with the dolphins.

It seems like it is better to avoid the noise and crowd of this commercial site by visiting the interesting **Cabrillo Marine Museum**. Although small, it gives a good impression of marine life of the local coast, 3720 Stephen White dr., San Pedro, tel. 548-7546. Admission free. Open Tues.-Fri. noon-5pm, weekends, 10am-5pm.

The **Port of Los Angeles** is located at San Pedro, squeezed in between the Palos Verdes Peninsula and Long Beach Harbor. The Long Beach and Los Angeles ports together handle an enormous amount of shipping. The **Los Angeles Maritime Museum** is located in the harbor itself, next to Ports of Call Village which is a shopping village. The museum is at the foot of 6th st., Berth 84, San Pedro. Open Tues.-Sun. 9:30am-5pm. Daily tours, tel. 548-7618. It gives a few glimpses of the American nautical past as well as the daily panorama of a huge bustling port.

**Long Beach**, at the southern end of Los Angeles County was for years seen only as an appendage to Los Angeles. It was a navy town, and facing Ocean Boulevard downtown were grease joints, corn dog stands, porno-movie theaters, sleazy clubs, and pawn shops. Near the water stood a rickety old amusement park. For about the past 15 years, Long Beach has steadily been transforming itself. Down came the sleazy bars and the amusement park along with the ornate turn-of-the-century architecture, and in their stead rose a wall of steel-and-glass towers.

Long Beach is one of the major ports on the West Coast and a rapidly growing shipping and oil center. The **Queen Mary** and the **Spruce Goose** (the biggest airplane in the world) have become centerpieces of a large tourist development scheme for the port and downtown area, which now has a large convention center and new hotels, and will soon have a new international trade center. For the business traveler, Long Beach offers the services, facilities and ambience of an urban center without the crowds and hassles of Los Angeles. Beyond the Queen Mary and Spruce Goose, there is little to keep the casual visitor enthralled. The beach area near Belmont Shore is a pleasant and convenient base for traveling to other points.

**The Queen Mary** comes from the age of pre-airline trans-Atlantic luxury travel, with care and class down to the doorknobs and marbled pillars. She was huge, longer than three American football fields laid end to end, and at the same time, the fastest ocean liner of the time. First, second and third-class passengers were clearly separated, with separate entrances. Third-class passengers were squeezed into the bow, which is the narrowest and most unstable part of the ship. When converted for wartime use as a troop carrier, over 15,000 soldiers were packed onto her decks, and Hitler offered a special reward for her sinking. She carried many famous and glamorous people, most notably Winston Churchill. Acquired by the city of Long Beach, she made her last voyage in 1967, docked in Long Beach Harbor, and is now a hotel and tourist attraction. Steeped in history, the Queen Mary developed its own folklore and mythology. During its refurbishing and when the hotel was first opened, stories of eerie incidents spread among workers and guards, such as reports of the lingering smell of cigar smoke near Winston Churchill's favorite lounge. Visitors can walk the length of the ship from bow to stern. A self-guided tour includes the enormous engine room and a slide show of the ship's history. Inquiring about a hotel room is worthwhile, if only to catch a glimpse of the beautiful polished lobby.

In the same complex as the Queen Mary, in a huge aluminum dome, sits the **Spruce Goose**, the world's largest airplane. The plane was intended to be a prototype for giant "flying boats" which would transport troops and equipment to Europe during World War II by air so as to avoid encounters with German U-boats. Howard Hughes, aviation engineer and pioneer, movie-maker, and flamboyant millionaire, backed the project. Against harsh criticism, Hughes determined to complete it, even when government enthusiasm waned. The plane was finally test-flown in Long Beach Harbor after the war by Hughes himself, who lifted it off the water for one mile. It was then returned to a hangar and kept hidden for 30 years.

Visitors can walk through the plane, and can also see exhibits about Hughes and the history of aviation. The most recent addition is the Time Voyager, which uses film, gravity, vibrations, visual effects, and goony dressed-up creatures to create the impression that you have penetrated time and galaxies. Queen Mary and Spruce Goose are at Pier J. Long, Long-Beach, open in summer 9am-8pm, shorter hours in winter, tel. 435-3511. $14.5 adult, $8.5 children 5-11, under 5 free.

Not far from the Spruce Goose is the **London Towne Village**, which is typical of southern California in that it is completely incongruous. Open all week, 10am-6pm in winter (box office closes at 4pm), and 9am-9pm between July 4th and Labor Day (box office closes at 8pm). Admission to the entire complex is quite steep, and it is not a bad idea to avoid this tourist trap to save time and money. In spite of its attractions it is a bit difficult to imagine Oliver Twist and Fagin dodging among the olde tourist shoppes, but if you want to check it out, tel. 435-3511.

The hub of Long Beach's refurbished downtown is a new but standard mall. One venerable institution remains, however. This is **Acres of Books**, on the east side of Long Beach blvd. between Broadway and 3rd, in a warehouse-sized used-book store that will lure and engulf book lovers. Pack a lunch.

Some fine temporary exhibits by modern regional artists pass through the **Long Beach Art Museum**, a small red brick building overlooking the sea by Bluff Park, 2300 Ocean blvd., tel. 439-2119.

Further east, follow Second St. to the **Belmont Shore** area, Long Beach's small beach town, with boutiques, coffeeshops, restaurants, and hip bars. A few blocks south is the beach and the Olympic-sized indoor swimming pool, which is open to the public. At the end of Belmont shore is a small library overlooking the Los Alomitos Bay, offering the perfect place to sit and browse through *Moby Dick*. Across the bay is **Naples**, a network of canals. The houses have big bay windows, a boat or two docked in front, and a car or two parked behind.

**Catalina Island**, 22 miles (35 km) off the Long Beach shore, provides a taste of exotic escape close to the mainland. **Avalon** is the only town on the island, and the remaining territory has been left in its natural state. Cars are rarely found — which in itself is a pleasant change of pace.

Passenger ferries, operated by *Catalina Cruises*, leave from both San Pedro and Long Beach. A round-trip costs $24.90 and allows about four hours on the island. Reservations are advisable, tel. 775-6111, or 514-3838.

The Visitor's Information and Service Center, at the pier, tel. 510-2500, and the Chamber of Commerce, tel. 510-1520, on Crescent ave. at the Pleasure Pier, can both provide information about island activities. The Chamber can also handle hotel bookings. Camping information and reservations can be made through the *Catalina Cove and Camp Agency*, tel. 510-0303.

Catalina is the place to give yourself totally to play. Bicycles, snorkels, scuba gear, kayaks and inner tubes can all be rented in Avalon. Cycling is an easy and beautiful way to explore the island. The town has two pretty sand beaches. The glass-bottom boat, gliding passengers across the undersea gardens filled with colorful fish and deep areas of seaweed, is a favorite and a highlight. If staying overnight in summer, take a night cruise in search of flying fish. The boat's searchlight disturbs the fish, and they leap past, sometimes over the boat.

Back in Avalon itself, stroll along Crescent ave. Fresh seafood is plentiful. The conspicuous art-deco building is the **Catalina Casino**, a movie theatre capped by a ballroom which once swung — and still does occasionally — to the big-band sound.

## Accommodations

### Expensive
*Hotel Queen Mary:* Pier J, P.O.Box 8, 90801, tel. 435-3511. The lobby has managed to preserve some of the ship's luxury, as so have some of the rooms, with porthole windows and original handles, faucets and so forth. Entrance to Queen Mary/Spruce Goose tours included. $64 up singles, $79 up doubles.
*Breakers Hotel:* 210 E. Ocean blvd., 90802, tel. 432-8781; toll-free US, tel. 800-221-5053; toll-free CA, tel. 800-221-8941. Downtown, overlooking the beaches and port, next to the Convention Center. An old ornate brick building, even more conspicious because all its old neighbors have been torn down. $70 up singles/doubles.

### Moderate
*City Center Motel:* 255 Atlantic ave. 90802, tel. 435-2483.

Downtown, near the Convention Center, reasonably priced for the area, with a pool. $38 singles, $46 doubles.

## Food

*Ly's Garden*: Broadway and Long Beach blvd. An all-you-can-eat Chinese lunch buffet for $3.25.

*Wongs*: 1506 E. Broadway. Serving delicious and filling cheap lunches, this is a popular local spot, along a mildy hip gay strip.

*Mardi Gras*: Shoreline Village: Wear your sunglasses here against the glare of the waiter's costumes and wall hangings. Overlooking the water, a popular spot with a bar/danceroom that hops. Huge portions of delicious food. Very reasonable.

*Hamburger Henry's*: 4700 E. 2nd st. In Belmont shore, an easy walk to the beach, this 24-hour local landmark has had a facelift bringing it back to the boppin' 50s. Hamburgers are delicious but not cheap.

*Jolly Rogers*: 130 Marina dr., Seaport Village. Located very near the Pacific Coast Highway, this would be your standard coffee shop but for two things; a pretty relaxing view over Alamitos Bay, and a great $1.50 happy hour with hors-d'oeuvres.

*Trader Joe's*: Marina Pacifica Mall, 2nd st. at Pacific coast Highway. A cut-rate gourmet deli and a great place to stock up for a picnic. There's always something interesting on sale here, whether it be cashew nuts, fancy mustard, protein powder or rum.

## Important addresses and phone numbers

Long Beach Convention and Visitors Council: 180 E. Ocean blvd., Suite 150, tel. 436-3645.

24-hour Events Line: tel. 499-7722.

*Greyhound*: 6601 N. Atlantic blvd., tel. 603-0141.

*Trailways*: 245 W. 3rd st., tel. 436-3231.

*Long Beach Transit*: tel. 591-2301. Efficient and modernized.

*RDT* Information: tel.639-6800. There is an express bus between downtown Long Beach and downtown L.A.

Long Beach Airport: 4100 Donald Douglas dr., tel. 421-8293. Can give information on carriers, schedules and ground transportation.

Airport Service: tel. 596-16662. Private bus service extending to John Wayne Airport and Disneyland in Orange County, and LAX.

# The South Coast

## Orange County

The development of Orange County creeps steadily along. The acres of orange groves have long since been uprooted. A bastion of arch-conservative politics (the *John Birch Society* is well-entrenched in local politics), the area is also a center for the sprouting of instant towns. The closest thing to a downtown is the newest shopping mall. Only along the coast have the towns clung to any sense of separate identity, and these are primarily enclaves for the affluent. Tourists come all over the world to visit Orange County's main attraction — Disneyland.

## Disneyland

Besides the beaches, the main reason to linger in Orange County is a visit to **Disneyland**. Opened in 1955, this 1950s vision of fantasy and the future, an amazing feat of imagination, still draws almost 12 million visitors a year. Even with the opening of Disneyworld in Florida, the original is still the number one place of fun.

Disneyland is located at 1313 Harbor Boulevard in Anaheim; you won't miss the signs, and the Matterhorn is visible from the street. It is open every day of the year, till midnight on Saturdays and Sundays, with extended opening hours in summertime and holiday seasons, tel. 714-999-4565 or 213-626-8605, ext. 4565, to check. Admission prices for adults: one day unlimited pass, $23.50; two days, $42.50; three days $56.50. Children: one day, $18.50; two days, $33.50; three days $44.50. There is a *Senior Fun Day Passport* for over 60s, Sun.-Fri., from September till June. It costs $18-75. There are also guided tours which last 3-4 hours and then give unlimited use of rides, at $33 for adults and $20 for children. If you can pass for under 12, you'll get in as a child, and if you pass for under 2 you'll get in for free.

Disneyland's excellence is embodied in the tremendous detail that has gone into its construction. The fantasy is complete in every facet. In Frontierland, every prop, down to the garbage cans, blends in with the wild west. In the Haunted House, even the spiders webs look real.

The park is divided into seven areas: **Adventureland**, **Critter Country**, **Fantasyland**, **Frontierland**, **Main Street USA**, **New Orleans Square**, and **Tomorrowland**. The main gate leads into Main Street, which is the trunk from which the other themelands branch out. The newest and fastest rideis **Splash Mountain** in **Critter Country**, which takes you through backwoods and swamps at top speeds of 40 miles (64 km) per hour, with a final big splash of a 45 degree 50 ft. (17 m) drop into a briar-filled pond. The **Disneyland Railroad** around the park's perimeter provides an overview. After the full circle, you can remain on board and disembark where you please.

Disneyland seems to have everything, including a place to park the kids and the dog, as well as feed the baby and change its diapers. The restaurants are very reasonably priced. They range from burger stands to an elegant full-course restaurant on a Louisiana bayou in perpetual night, complete with fireflies.

Among the best adventures in Disneyland, in addition to **Splash Mountain**, are **Its a Small World** and **Peter Pan's Flight** (Fantasy Land), **Star Tours** and the 3-dimentional movie in the **Magic Eye Theater** (Tomorrow Land), **Jungle Cruise** (Adventure Land) and the Happy Parades in the main street.

You will easily spend a full day here, and you will need more than one if you want to see everything. During the summer the lines for popular attractions can easily be over an hour long. With extended hours during the summer, you might consider arriving in the late afternoon, when the heat and crowds begin to ease, and staying late. Actually, one of the best days you can choose for Disneyland is Christmas, when you can practically walk right into any ride or show without waiting at all. If you wish to leave Disneyland and return to it on the same day, don't forget to get your hand stamped at the exit.

To reach Disneyland by car, exit south on Harbor Blvd. from the Santa Anna Freeway, or north from the Garden Grove Freeway. Disneyland is accessible by public bus from downtown Los Angeles, Long Beach and various points in Orange County. Check with the appropriate municipal bus system for details. The *Gray Line* offers Disneyland tours, and Airport Service connects with Disneyland from the Los Angeles, Long Beach and John Wayne airports.

### Knott's Berry Farm

Knott's Berry Farm, in Buena Park, is older and larger than Disneyland, but its upstart neighbor left it far behind. It is located at 8039 Beach blvd, Buena Park. Open in summer, Sun.-Fri. 9am-midnight, Sat. 9am-1am. Winter hours, Mon.-Fri. 10am-6pm, Sat. 10am-10pm, Sun. 10am-7pm. Call to verify. Admission $16.95, discounts for children 3-11 and for seniors, tel. 714-220-5200 or 714-220-5133 (public relations). Originally a berry farm, this amusement park still emphasizes the old-time rural flavor, and the tone is one of nostalgia for Americana.

There is the hold-up of the **Butterfield Stagecoach**, **Bigfoot Rapid** an exhilarating ride down a raging white-water river, and a recreated **Fiesta Village** and **Roaring Twenties** scenario. Some of the rides, such as the roller-coaster called **Montezooma's Revenge**, are real stomach turners. The park's restaurant has good, reasonably priced fried chicken dinners.

The two other attractions of Buena Park, the **Movieland Wax Museum** (7711 Buena Park Blvd., tel. 714-522-1155) and the **Museum of World Wars** (tel. 714-952-1776) are nothing to write home about and might be given-up for the beautiful beaches.

Newport Beach is a few miles north of Laguna Beach, separated by a long open stretch of beach. The bay between the narrow **Balboa Peninsula** and the mainland is a beautiful harbor filled with pleasure crafts gleaming in the dark blue waters. Along the

**Fantasy at Disneyland**

extremely narrow peninsula is a cluster of trendy bars, eateries and shops in a simulated old-time carnival surrounding. The streets and wharfside walks are bedecked with lights on a summer evening and filled with young people whose tans seem to shine in the dark. A vintage ferry makes the short run between the peninsula and **Balboa Island**, where a few more cafes and restaurants line the street, and expensive houses are packed tightly together. Costing a mere 20 cents per standing passenger, the ride is refreshing and especially beautiful on a balmy summer night when the strings of multi-colored lights are reflected upon the water.

The Balboa Peninsula's famous **Wedge** is a section of beach that draws 10-foot waves, surfers who challenge them, and spectators who hang-on vicariously. To feel the surge and rush of the ocean around you, walk out toward the end of the long rock breakwater extending from the end of the peninsula.

**Huntington Beach** has been the cutting edge of California's surf scene ever since the days of the Beach Boys. To this day, brightly-painted surfboard shops line the coastal highway, and barefoot kids in bathing suits ride their bicycles clasping their boards under their arms. The beach at night still sparkles with bonfires, and the bar scene is still young and rowdy. Up-and-coming bands, purple haired and dressed to match, play new wave music.

For the more sedate, strolling to the end of **Huntington Pier** is a popular past-time. At the end is the appropriately named **End Cafe**, a nice place to sit, have a bite, sip coffee and gaze at the sun as it sets.

## Accommodations
### Around Disneyland

*Disneyland Hotel*: (150 W. Cerritos ave., 92082, tel. 714-778-6600 or 800-MICKEY-1). The expensive hotel is the official Disneyland hotel. Their special package includes the dream of every child, an unlimited entry permit to Disneyland while staying at the hotel.

There are plenty of motels around Disneyland. Almost all the national chains are represented here from the inexpensive **Motel 6** (the closest one to Disneyland is on 921 S. Beach Blvd., tel. 714-220-2866) to the better ones.

**Camping**: Koa has a site close by for vans and trailer homes. This place is always full, so you better reserve well ahead. Koa, 1221 S. West st., Anaheim, LA, 92082.

### Beaches

*Huntington Shore Motor Hotel*, 21002 Pacific Coast Hwy, tel. 714-536-8861. Expensive but very nice with beautiful ocean views. Highly recommended if you can afford it.

*Huntington Beach Hostel*, 421, 8th st., tel. 714-536-3315. Great hostel. Call for reservation in advance. $9 per night.

# Laguna Beach

Laguna Beach, famous for its art colony, elegance, and stunning cliff and beach, is the main attraction on the coast between San Diego and Los Angeles. The high chaparral hills here slope down to a line of bluffs, beaches and coves.

Perched in the hills are gorgeous homes, matched only by the those built into the bluffs above the beaches. Along the Pacific Coast Highway and its side streets are clusters of galleries, shops, restaurants and hotels. Sea breezes temper the summer heat, and in winter the temperature rarely drops below 50°F (10°C).

## How to get there

The coastal approach to Laguna Beach is pretty and hilly from both north and south, and punctuated with state beaches. From the north, this route can become congested as far south as Newport Beach during the afternoon rush hours. For a faster route from Los Angeles, take I-5 south (called the Santa Anna Freeway in the L.A. region) and exit west on Laguna Canyon Road, which winds through some gentle hills into town. By freeway, Laguna Beach is little more than an hour from Los Angeles, and just over half-an-hour from Disneyland. Laguna Beach is a lovely place for a relaxing evening after a full day's stimulation in the magic kingdom.

The *Laguna Beach Municipal Transit System* reaches the beaches and major points in town. During the summer festival season, special tram routes connect the various parking lots with the town.

Thousands of visitors flock to the town in July and August for the Laguna Beach *Festival of Arts*. Launched during the Depression as a desperate move by local struggling artists to arouse interest in their work, the festival has since become an established local institution. The festival includes the *Pageant of the Masters*, in which local residents pose in live versions of great artistic masterpieces. If you are an art lover, don't miss the **Laguna Beach Museum of Art** which has two locations on 307 Cliff Drive (tel. 714-494-6531) and at South Coast Plaza (tel. 714-662-3366). In these museums you can see contemporary American art and changing exhibits.

Concurrently held are the *Sawdust Festival* (which began as an alternative to the main festival and places emphasis on crafts) and **Art-a-Fair**. It seems that on every holiday there is some sort of art or crafts fair.

The whole town buzzes during the festival season and the galleries and studios do a brisk business. A large concentration of them are found on the 300 block of the North Coast Highway. On the first Saturday of every month a **Gallery Row Art Walk** is held on this block between 4-7pm, where one can meet local artists. Refreshments are usually served.

Unlike the beach cities to the north and south, Laguna Beach is not just one stretch of beach. Its beaches are separate scalloped strands, with coves, cliffs, tide pools and arches carved by the waves. The surf and wave conditions vary from beach to beach.

One of the prettiest is **Crescent Bay** near the northern boundary at the end of Crescent Bay dr. (turn west at the 76 gasoline station). Steep stairs lead down to a secluded beach with tide pools at the northern end.

Further south, **Heisler Park** has winding footpaths among beautiful flowers. The paths follow the bluffs and provide a great overlook for the setting sun. Toward the end of December, this is a popular spot for watching the grey whales as they migrate south from the Arctic region.

From the center of town, where Broadway meets the coast highway, the south shore is lined with restaurants and hotels. **Victoria Beach**, toward the southern end of town, is a secluded public beach that is often almost empty. The tall tower, that looks as if has been transplanted from a medieval castle, houses a spiral staircase for a house atop the cliff. Park on the highway by Victoria drive and follow the street to the steep stairs descending to the beach.

## Accommodations

Pleasant lodgings can be found in town, but they are fairly expensive. For higher standards and less expensive motels, head north or south of town, or inland toward the freeways and the more suburban areas of Orange County.

The closest beach camping is found in the south, at three state beaches in the area of Dana Point and San Clemente. These, however, tend to be crowded.

*Casa Laguna Inn*: 2510 S. Coast Highway, Laguna Beach 92651, tel. 714-494-2996. Toll-free in-state, tel. 1-800-233-0449. A small verdant maze of balconies and patios, this B&B inn at the south end of town is very classy. Each room is furnished differently. Breakfasts are home-made. There are many personal touches, such as complimentary afternoon tea and wine. It is located near secluded Victoria Beach. Starting at $85 single/double. For a weekly stay, the last night is complimentary.

*Hotel Laguna*: 425 S. Coast Highway, Laguna Beach 92651, tel. 714-494-1151. Toll-free in-state, tel. 1-800-524-2927. Located in the center of town, right on the beach, this old hotel is a local historic landmark. Many rooms overlook the beach. Some are a bit more plain than the exterior would suggest. The location is unbeatable. Starting at $65 single, $75 double.

**Laguna Beach — Sun, sand and sea**

## Food

Laguna Beach has the atmosphere of a Mediterranean resort. With a daily influx of beach-goers, there are many elegant seaside restaurants, pizza stands and delis, plus as many brands of frozen yogurt as you'll see in one place.

*The White House*, 340 So. Coast Highway, tel. 494-8089. Terrific early bird specials include baked fish, lamb, chicken teriyaki or other main courses, with all the trimmings and a glass of wine, for $7.95.

*Renaissance Bakery and Coffee House*, 234 Forest ave. The blintzes, piroshkis, strudels and borscht create a touch of Europe in the California sun. A nice place to sip a cappuccino and watch the people go by.

## Important addresses and phone numbers

Area Code: 714.
Emergency: 911.
Chamber of Commerce: 357 Glenneyre St., tel. 494-1018. This town churns out the public relations brochures and weekly visitor papers. Check through them for discount coupons for restaurants.

*Laguna Beach Municipal Transit*: tel. 497-3311, ext. 246.
*Orange County Transit District*: tel. 636-RIDE.

## San Juan Capistrano

North of Camp Pendleton and San Clemente (home of Richard Nixon's "Western White House") are San Juan Capistrano and Dana Point. **Mission San Juan Capistrano**, built in 1777, is famous for its legendary swallows. The swallows return each year at the beginning of March. The complex is set around two colorful, peaceful courtyards. The seventh mission in Father Junipero Serra's chain of missions, it mission includes the **Serra Chapel**, the oldest building in California and the only chapel in which it is known that Serra officiated, located at 31882 Camino Capistrano. Open 7am-5pm, $2 admission, tel. 714-493-1424.

The nearby old **Santa Fe Depot** is used today by *Amtrak*. The old fixtures, railroad cars and even the advertisements have been preserved, and a bar has been opened. Between the station and the mission is the *Green Burrito*, a small stand serving delicious and filling meals.

The harbor at **Dana Point** is well-known among fishermen. **Dana Wharf** also has a protected beach especially good for young children. For the first three weekends in February, the *Dana Point Harbor Festival of Whales* has various programs and tours to celebrate the southern migration of the grey whales.

## The Mountain Rim

The Los Angeles Basin is rimmed on the north and east by the **San Gabriel** and **San Bernardino Mountains**, respectively. A little further to the southeast are the **San Jacintos** (see "Palm Springs"). The first two ranges, especialy the San Gabriels, literally loom at the edge of the urban area. These ranges not only create the barrier which divides the dry basin from the true desert, but also constitute an alpine world in themselves. The lower ranges may be closed in summer due to fire hazard. This immediate proximity of true wilderness is partly what makes the L.A. region so appealing, and what makes the immense city of Los Angeles so different from other major urban centers such as New York or Chicago. Both these mountains ranges boast peaks thrusting up over 10,000 feet (3,400 m).

There is space to ride and hike, fish and hunt, and find solitude and undisturbed nature at the very edge of the city. Both the San Gabriel and San Bernardino ranges have become popular ski resorts in winter, even while people are surfing down below. Lift tickets often sell out. They can be bought in advance from *Ticketron*, which adds on a charge. Night skiing can often be a little cheaper. For ski resort information, contact the Big Bear Chamber of Commerce (see below).

The San Gabriels sit right behind Pasadena and other northern communities of the L.A. basin. The high country contains pine forests, waterfalls, rugged hiking trails and ski resorts. Much of the region is included in the **Angeles National Forest**. Trails in the front range are easily accessible from the cities below. An exceptionally rugged portion has been preserved as the **San Gabriel Wilderness Area**, with steep slopes and canyons and trails to challenge experienced hikers.

For more information on the National Forest area write to: The Angeles National Forest, N. Lake ave., Pasadena 91104.

For the best view of these mountains you can get without hiking far, follow the Angeles Crest Highway, from La Canada.

San Bernardino is higher than San Gabriel. **Mt. San Gorgonio** reaches over 11,500 feet (3,900 m). San Bernardinos is popular and developed and is crowded during both summer vacations and winter ski season. There are many ski-areas here. **Lake Arrowhead** and **Big Bear Lake** are artificially created lakes which are surrounded by little resort towns and camping areas. The Rim of the World Drive, Highway 18, follows the ridges past some spectacular views. It ends with a loop around Big Bear Lake. Alternately, one can continue along Route 18 and wind ones way into the desert.

The Big Bear Chamber of Commmerce and the Big Bear Lake Tourist and Visitor Bureau can provide information on hiking, skiing, camping, etc. The Chamber of Commerce will also provide hotel or chalet information and can arrange reservations.

Big Bear Chamber of Commerce: P.O. Box 2860, Big Bear Lake, 92315, tel. 714-866-4601.

Big Bear Lake Tourist and Visitor Bureau: P.O. Box 3050G, Big Bear Lake 92315, tel. 714-866-5878.

# Inland Southern California

Most of the tourists follow the highway 1 route along the coast between L.A. and San Francisco but there is still a lot more to see in the area inland. Here one can see agricultural cities in the fertile San Joaquin Valley or majesic national parks in the Sierra Nevada Range.

## San Joaquin Valley

*California is a Garden of Eden,*
*It's a Paradise to live in or see,*
*But believe it or not, you won't find it so hot*
*If you ain't got the Do Re Mi*
                    Woody Guthrie

The San Joaquin Valley is a great, elongated, flat expanse of farmland and prairie running north-south through the center of the state. It merges with the Sacramento Valley in the north to form one long strip of fertile farmland. Far more compact than the sprawling grainfields of the American Midwest, and fed by the waters of the Sierras, this rich valley produces one-sixth of America's agricultural produce.

This is the state's heartland, but it is the place that everyone passes through and no one lingers in. Motorists between San Francisco and Los Angeles race along Interstate 5 at the western rim to avoid the slower coastal routes.

I-80 leads through the valley towards the ski slopes, resorts and casinos of Tahoe and Reno. Government workers enter and leave Sacramento through it, and hikers use its eastern roads to penetrate the Sierras.

This seemingly pastoral valley has witnessed some of California's most dramatic social struggles. In this valley the railroads, with their vast land holdings, were pitted against the farmers and ranchers at the turn of the century. Through the writings of John Steinbeck, notably in *The Grapes of Wrath*, the entire American nation learned of the plight of the Oakies, the Dust Bowl refugees from the great plains who, during the 1930s, crossed the desert and over the California hills by their thousands, seeking work, sustenance and land, only to be held back by the controlling interests and their hired gangs.

The racial bias of many Californians against Chinese, Japanese,

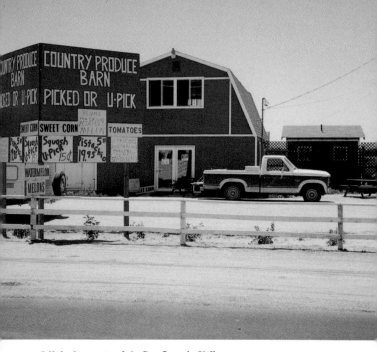

*Off the beaten track in San Joaquin Valley*

Mexican and Philippino farmworkers were highlighted in the central valley. They were exploited, paid sub-standard wages and lived in appalling living conditions. They were also accused of stealing American jobs and introducing strange foreign customs.

Even today, farm labor imported from Mexico — cheap, exploited and often illegal — has become a highly-charged issue. Immigrants from more distant places, such as Portugal and Southeast Asia, have also settled here. Some 40,000-50,000 Laotian Hmong are gaining a foothold in both farming and town occupations. These immigrants will eventually bring major changes to the tight traditional social fabric here.

The agricultural nature of the land itself is facing great challenges. High-tech industries have moved in, attracted by the research centers at Davis and the expanding urban centers of Sacramento, Fresno and Bakersfield. Sacramento, once viewed as an absurd site for the State Capital, is developing its own urban outskirts towards the Sierra foothills, and toward the west, where suburban development is already spilling over from the Bay Area, as housing costs skyrocket there. An increasing number of farm towns face the question of whether to retain their rural character, or to become amorphous commuter towns.

Urban expansion would sacrifice thousands of acres of prime farmland, at a time when California agriculture is already feeling the recession that has hit American agriculture in general. The valley holds a sixth of all the irrigated cropland in the U.S., but in the last five years the state's agricultural exports have shrunk by a third, and smaller countries are taking over the leadership from California in the marketing of certain crops. Not since the Great Depression have there been so many farm sales and mortgage foreclosures. When the banks resell the land, the speculators, developers, huge combines and foreign investors have a chance to move in and remove it from farm production.

The casual traveler, however, who finds the time to leave the freeways to follow the flat grid of backroads, will find that this is still the traditional countryside. Even a short detour may bring some pleasant surprises. Here you'll find old brick railroad stations, and diners where you'll discover some home-fried bargains (you might also end up with plain grease, but that's part of the game). Here you'll pass farm boys in their trucker caps driving tractors on the road, waitresses with bee-hive hairdos and country drawls, and billboards advertising cattle feed or urging repentance. This is the land of county fairs and barbecues, 4-H clubs and local rodeos. Bullfights are held at Escalon, on Route 120, south of Stockton, (along one route to Yosemite).

The valley is steeped in the sounds and smells of farm production, every season with its particular signs. During winter, it's the fermenting residue of beet processing, and the gins and ragged white debris of cotton-picking; in spring there is the successive blossoming of almond, cherry, peach and plum trees; and the autumn air fills with the pungent sweetness of the grape harvest. Then there is the thick odor of the peat land, the smell of onions and fertilizer, the gold of endless fields of grain and the dairy cattle grazing in the low eastern hills.

**How to get there**
The main towns and cities of the valley, Bakersfield, Fresno, Merced, Modesto, Stockton and Sacramento are connected by the 99 Freeway, which runs north-south along the eastern fringe. I-5 parallels Route 99, along the western rim. It continues north beyond Sacramento, into the narrowing Sacramento Valley and climbs into the Shasta range. The valley cities often serve as stopovers en route to the Sierras. *Greyhound*, *Trailways* and *Amtrak* link the main cities.

## Bakersfield

Near the southern point of the valley, **Bakersfield** is separated from the L.A. metropolis by the bare and rocky Tehachapi range and its winding Grapevine pass. Bakersfield has its own countrified sprawl, with gas stations and fast-food stands spreading towards the flat horizon. Recreation opportunities lie to the east, along Route 178. **Sequoia National Forest** covers the southern extremity of the Sierras, south of Sequoia National Park. Through this area the churning, twisting Kern River offers whitewater rafting. Lake Isabella, on the Kern, is the recreation center in the area. There is abundant free camping in the National Forest.

Route 178 continues east past Lake Isabella and provides a magnificent, if leisurely, route for crossing the Sierras. It climbs to well over 5,000 feet at Walker Pass, and then drops along the steep eastern slope to the Owens Valley beyond.

Along Highway 99 there are numerous motels, ranging from cheap (under $25) to overpriced. Unless you can be lulled to sleep by the roar of trucks at midnight, check the room's noise level first if you are pulling off the highway for a snooze.

### Important addresses and phone numbers

Area Code: 805.
Chamber of Commerce: 1033 Truxtun, 8:30am-5pm, tel. 327-4421.
Kern City Board of Trade: 2101 Oak st., 8am-5pm, tel. 861-2367. Lots of information.
US Forest Service, Greenhorn District: 800 Truxtan, Rm 322, 8am-5pm, tel. 861-4212. Details on camping and hiking in the Sierra National Forest.
*Amtrak*: 15th & 1st., tel. 327-7863.
*Greyhound*: 1820 18th st., tel. 327-7371. Service to L.A. and valley cities.
*Trailways*: 1821 18th st., tel. 327-7961.
*Golden Empire Transit*: tel. 327-7686.
City-wide system.

## Visalia

North of Bakersfield, Visalia is the starting or finishing point for trips into **Sequoia National Park**, especially the southern part which includes the backpacking paradise of Mineral King. The park lies about an hour away. The road heading east from town has a few cheap motels. You will find camping spots in the vicinity of Lake Kaweah, before you get to the national park itself. Groceries are cheaper here than in the park. Visalia is on the main train and bus stops (though the *Amtrak* station is in adjacent Hanford), but transit to Sequoia is abysmal to non-existent.

If, after a week of eating powdered eggs and oatmeal in the back country, you crave a taste of decadence, head for *Mearle's Drive-in*, on Route 63 between Vesalia and Tulare. The huge blinking milkshake on the roof will be your beacon. On Friday night cars and pick-ups surround the place, which is filled with old couples out on the town, farm families and young bucks with squeaky-clean dates. In the age of designer ice cream cones, this throwback sells delicious old-fashioned cones for 50-85 cents. *Pita Mania*, at 225 Main at Eccina, serves huge lunches for $3.

### Important addresses and phone numbers
Area Code: 209.
Convention and Visitors Bureau: 720 W. Mineral King, Visalia 93291, tel. 734-5876. This office will help you plan your visit to Sequoia and Kings Canyon National Parks, especially what it calls a *48 Hour Mini Vacation*. Some discount coupons are included.
*Greyhound*: 211 S. Court st., tel. 734-3507.
*Amtrak* (Hanford): tel. 800-872-7245.

## Fresno

Fresno is the financial center of the San Joaquin Valley, as well as the junction for several routes into the Sierras. Route 41 heads to Yosemite, Route 180 goes south-east to Sequoia/Kings Canyon, and Route 168 winds east into the Sierra National Forest. *Amtrak* and the two major bus companies serve the city.

Fresno has a rich ethnic fabric. Its well-settled Armenian population produced the great writer William Saroyan. Chinese, Japanese, Basque and Chicano communities have moved in, and the city is now the center for the waves of Laotian Hmongs who have moved into the valley.

The old Chinatown, along Kern st by G, F and E st., is a good place for Mexican, Japanese and other ethnic food. The farmer's market, on Divisadero st. at Route 41 has some fine local produce, as does the outdoor market held at the corner of Merced and N sts., on Tuesday, Thursday and Saturday from 7am-3pm.

You'll probably only be passing through Fresno, but you might stop at the **Storyland**, 890 W. Belmont ave. Open daily June-Sept. 10am-5pm. Off-season, during weekends and holidays. Admission charged, tel. 264-2235. This is a good place to stretch up if you have children with you. This place has slides, carousels and a place for a picnic in **Roeding Park**.

The **Hmong Craft Shop**, a non-profit shop, displays some exquisite quilts, wall hangings and other pieces made by some 300 Laotian craftswomen, 842 N. Fulton. Open Tues-Fri. 10am-4pm, Sat. 10am-2pm, tel. 237-7106.

The **Discovery Center** is a hands-on science museum and outdoor center with a laser phone among its high-tech toys, 1944 N. Winery. Open Tues.-Fri. 11am-5pm, tel. 251-5531. Admission.

## Important addresses and phone numbers
Area Code: 209.
Convention and Visitor Bureau: 690 M st., tel. 233-2630.
*Greyhound*: 1033 Broadway, tel. 268-9461.
*Trailways*: 1333 Broadway, tel. 237-7181.
*Amtrak*: Tulare & Q., tel. 252-8253.
Hospital: Fresno Community Medical Center, Fresno and R st., tel. 442-6000.

# Sierra Nevada

*Then it seemed to me the Sierra Nevada should be called not the Nevada or the Snowy Range, but the Range of Light. And after ten years spent in the heart of it... it still seems to me, above all others, the Range of Light is the most divinely beautiful of all the mountain chains I have ever seen.*

John Muir

The Sierra Nevada, east of the great San Joaquin and Sacramento Valleys, forms a solid granite mass running some 400 miles from the area of Plumas county in the north to the Tahachapis and the Mojave Desert in the south. So sharply do the eastern and western slopes differ, that it is hard to picture them forming the same system. The range of vegetation , wildlife and landscape in the Sierras is almost incomprehensible. From the east, the hills rise gently from the central valley, through the chaparral and grass covered foothils, the legendary gold country. Along a 60 mile (96 km) stretch, these gentle slopes rise toward the high country. The high country, the jagged north-south spine of the mountains etched with canyons and meadows, with peaks ranging from 7,000 to 15,000 feet (2,400 m to 5,100 m) high, can be crossed only through a few passes, and has a winter season with up to 20-30 feet (7 m to 10 m) of snow and which lasts from November to July. On the east, these peaks drop precipitously. Moist winds from the Pacific bring rain to the western slopes, but the eastern escarpment get very little rain, and the vegetation is semi-desert, blending into the desert itself. The view which faced pioneers more than a century ago, was of a solid, impenetrable granite wall. Many settlers lost their lives trying to haul their wagons and cattle up these almost impassable inclines. Even today, with super-highways blasted through the granite and powerful autos, maneuvering along these ridges and passes can be hazardous.

These mountains, with their sharply contrasting environments, support a tremendous variety of plant and animal life. Their western slopes provide the only habitat for the largest living organisms on earth, the giant sequoia trees. The ranges just east of the Sierras contain another unique ecological habitat containing the oldest

*Winter in the Sierra Nevada*

trees on earth, the bristlecone pines, some of which are over 4,000 years old.

Both the eastern and western slopes of this massive range contain gold, as well as other minerals. The forests have provided huge amounts of lumber, game and pelts. The western foothills, in addition to gold, provided grazing land and orchards. Along the entire length of the range, rains and melted snows have made the central valley the richest agricultural basin in the country, and have supplied San Fransisco Bay with fresh water.

The fantastic recreation opportunities comprise an equally precious resource. The fishing, camping, hiking, boating, downhill and cross-country skiing are all superb. Whether your taste is for gambling in the carnival-like casinos on the Nevada border, or for hiking on the unsurpassed Pacific Crest Trail (which runs from Mexico to Canada), there is something for everyone in these mountains, and sometimes it seems that everyone rushes up together on one weekend. The resorts are crowded, the traffic can get tangled and the campgrounds resemble suburban blocks excised from L.A. and dropped down here in the wilderness. There is steady pressure for more development and more resorts, as well as more tree-cutting, dam-building, and the continued channeling of river courses. As recently as ten years ago, there was an almost successful proposal to blast a freeway through the supposedly inviolate borders of Sequoia National Park in order to develop a ski resort.

Despite the crowds and pressures to develop the area, the Sierras can still provide the kind of majesty, inspiration and peace that John Muir described a century ago — you just have to look a bit harder these days.

## The Amazing Sequoia Tree

Bordered by desert, high plateaus and the ocean, California has developed some unique ecological features. Ways of life that disappeared from other regions of the world found small pockets of protection here. Conspicuous among these is the Giant Sequoia.

These trees stand alone as the largest living things on earth. Though tall, they are not the tallest, and though old, they are not the oldest. But for sheer overall bulk, nothing is larger. They can approach or exceed 300 feet (100 m) in height, the length of an American football field, and their circumference can reach 100 feet. These massive trees are supported by roots that are only several feet deep, but, like long sinewy fingers, they grip the surface in every direction for up to 100 (34 m) feet. High and mighty as they are, these trees live delicately balanced lives. Some have reached an age of 3,200 years, and when the Greek and Hebrew civilizations were just beginning to develop, some of these trees were saplings in the same forests we can visit today. The sequoia, the coastal redwoods, and a single tree in China are all that remain of a family of trees that once covered the earth.

When the Giant Sequoias were first discovered, efforts immediately began to both exploit and protect them. Early lumbermen fashioned special saws and techniques to down the thick trees, some of which have girths approaching 30 feet (10 m). A branch alone may be six feet (2 m) thick. But the brittleness of the wood, and the height from which the trees fell, made efforts to harvest them impractical. Its cousin, the coastal redwood, was not so lucky.

Though the huge trees were protected, their delicately balanced ecology was little understood. For years, anxious rangers snuffed out forest fires to protect the trees, only to realize at last that fire played an essential role in the growth process of the sequoias. Fire prepares the soil for optimal sprouting, and clears the debris so that the tiny seed can reach the soil. Fire pops the seed from a closed cone, and also burns off young fir trees that grow in the shade and crowd out the sequoia seedlings. The mature trees have a thick, soft, fibrous bark up to two feet (70 cm) thick, that acts as a natural asbestos and insulates the tree from fire when other trees are destroyed. Even when, over many years, successive fires caused by accumulated debris burn through and perhaps hollow out a sequoia, the tree can continue to grow.

The sequoia tree was named by an Austrian botanist to honor an obscure intellectual giant, the great Cherokee Indian, Sequoya. A crippled mechanic and an artist, Sequoya invested 12 years of intellectual labor developing a system of English notation for Cherokee syllables, thus opening a whole world of literacy and literature for the Cherokee, who had already successfully adopted the White civilization. This did not prevent their removal to the west in a grueling march at Bayonet Point, that killed thousands. Sequoya joined his people in their exile and devoted himself to the search for a common Indian grammar.

## Kings Canyon and Sequoia National Parks

Some of the most magnificent scenery in all the Sierras is found in the southern reaches of the range, in **Kings Canyon and Sequoia National Parks.** The largest of the Giant Sequoias, are found here in dense groves with hundreds of trees. Here the peaks of the high country reach 12,000-14,000 feet (4,000-4,800 m), and Mt. Whitney reaches almost 15,000 feet (5,100 m). So rugged are the mountains here that no road traverses the entire park, and access is from the west only. Kings Canyon and Sequoia form one continuous strip along the Sierra range, but no road joins them directly.

There is no direct route between the Yosemite and Sequoia parks. Motorists must drive to Fresno, and then back into the Sierras in

*The gigantic Sequoia*

## KINGS CANYON
## AND SEQUOIA NATIONAL PARK

a long wide V, and this discourages many visitors from going to Sequoia after Yosemite. Besides, they've already seen the big trees in Yosemite, and the spectacular Yosemite Valley. Sequoia, then, is not nearly as crowded as Yosemite. There is no built-up area as there is in Yosemite Valley. The tourist services blend in much more subtly with the setting, and the beauty is spectacular. Kings Canyon was praised by John Muir as even more beautiful than Yosemite.

Sequoia became a national park in 1890, the same year as Yosemite.

**General Grant National Park**, also established that year, protected the Grant Grove of sequoias and the surrounding area. In 1940, Kings Canyon was established, incorporating the General Grant Park.

From Route 99 in the San Joaquin Valley, the main routes entering the parks are Route 198 from Visalia in the southwest, or 180 from Fresno in the northwest. Fresno and Visalia can be reached easily enough without a car, but transportation to and within the national parks is difficult without a car. Major airlines serve Fresno, bus companies serve Fresno and Visalia. *Amtrak* serves Fresno and Hanford near Visalia. Rent-a+car service is available for the parks from Fresno or Visalia. Guest Services, the concessionaire with a monopoly on Sequoia food and lodging, operates a mini-bus between Fresno and various visitor centers (and their own lodges) in both parks, for a rather high price of around $15.

## Kings Canyon National Park

Route 180 from Fresno enters **Kings Canyon National Park** at **Grant Grove**, which is separate from and west of the main body of the park. From here, a road leads east into Kings Canyon. The 46-mile (74-km) General's Highway leads south to sequoia, past the park's most renowned sights.

Grant Grove contains a visitor center, a small commercial center, and the grove itself. The visitor center offers films and very good displays about the evolution and life-cycle of the sequoia, as well as the attempts to fell them and to save them. Grant Grove contains site four of the world's five largest trees. The **Grant Tree**, a national shrine, is between 2,000 and 2,500 years old. There are several famous trees here, in addition to stumps left where trees were cut down by early loggers. There are pleasant short hikes within and around the grove. A longer 10-mile (16 km) loop goes to **Redwood Grove** to the south, a beautiful and less crowded grove.

The main and only highway winding into the heart of Kings Canyon Park ends in **Cedar Grove**. The canyon is stunning and overpowering as your car weaves at the base of its massive, granite walls. The canyon is 8,000 feet (2,700 m) deep, the deepest in the U.S. Just outside the park border is **Boyden Cavern**, a commercially developed cave with beautiful stalagmite and stalactite formations. It is more expensive ($3) and commercial than Crystal Cave, which is in Sequoia Park towards the southern end.

Cedar Grove has some visitor facilities, including campgrounds and several stores. Trails to **Zumwalt Meadows** and **Roaring River Falls** make easy and pretty hikes. Cedar Grove is a hub for trails penetrating the high country to the east and north. One beautiful all-day hike leads to **Mist Falls**. The **John Muir Trail**, which starts at Mt. Whiney, passes through Cedar Grove and extends as far as the large wilderness in the northern park of Kings Canyon Park. This trail runs along the crest of the Sierra to Tuolumne Meadows in Yosemite. It is for experienced hikers and needs some advance planning. Nevertheless, those willing to put in the planning, time and effort will get an incomparable feel for these mountains.

Cedar Grove's four campgrounds are generally open from late April to late October, as weather permits. Food service, laundry, showers and horseback riding are available. Reservations are recommended for the lodge.

## Sequoia National Park

From Grant Grove, the **General's Highway** leads into Sequoia National Park. You can follow this past the main sequoia groves, all the way to the southern end of the park.

**Redwood Canyon**, along General's Highway about four-and-a+half miles (7 km) southwest of Grant Grove, can be reached by foot (the trailhead is by **Quail's Flat**). Located in a small valley, it contains one of the more pristine sequoia groves and is one of the few places where you can camp out under the huge trees. The highway continues south, past the **Lodgepole Visitors' Center** which is an excellent source of information about the park, before heading to **Giant Forest**. Between Lodgepole and Giant Forest, along the General's Highway, are some of the finest groups of sequoia, as well as the largest concentration of visitor facilities and crowds. Also found here, between the two points, is a fine network of trails for pleasant day hikes. Some of the most popular are the **Lakes Trail** from Lodgepole, the **Congress Trail** from the General Sherman tree, and the hike to **Morro Rock** offering an expansive view of the western peaks and the San Joaquin Valley. The various trails allow the casual visitor and hiker to take routes as easy and short, or long and strenuous, as he wants.

Horseback riding is available at the **Wolverton Pack Station**, south of Lodgepole, tel. 565-3445. Downhill ski and snow play areas are also found at Wolverton. The ski season runs from about December through April. Cross-country ski touring centers around **Grant Forest Village**.

The Giant Forest contains the **General Sherman tree**, which is the largest of the sequoias, making it the largest living thing on earth. In the same grove are other sequoias, slightly smaller but still huge and impressive.

The drive to **Crescent Meadow** includes the auto log and tunnel. John Muir called this meadow the gem of the Sierras.

South of the Giant Forest, just past the **Guardsman Trees**, is the turnoff for **Crystal Cave**, a cavern featuring stalactites, stalagmites and an underground stream. Guided tours leave every hour from 10am-3pm, through to about mid-September. Arrive at the parking

*A green meadow in a lush forest*

lot at least 15 minutes before the tour, as it is a half-mile strenuous walk to the cave entrance from the parking lot. The cave is a breezy 48°F (9°c) so bring a jacket or sweater. Admission charged.

South of Crystal Cave is the **Eleven Range Overlook**, which really does seem to overlook layer upon layer of shaded mountainous horizon toward the west. From this point the road winds precipitously downwards from the glades of giant trees to sparse chaparral country, still within the park. At the southern end are the park headquarters at **Ash Mountain**, and several campgrounds. Just outside the park, at the hamlet of Hammond, is the road leading back into the park, specifically to the wilderness at Mineral King.

## Mineral King

**Mineral King** is a pristine alpine meadow toward the southern end of Sequoia, reached by an extremely winding road that should only be attempted in cars in good condition. Allow one-and-a+half hours to negotiate the 25-mile (40 km) route. The effort is worthwhile. Here, you stand in high alpine meadows, isolated from the rest of the park, with trails climbing steeply from the valley floor to the high lake basins around you. At **Silver City**, a private community along the road within the park, there are limited facilities including cabins, food, gas and groceries. A park station near the Mineral King ranger station arranges day rides and pack trips.

Mineral King was little-known and little used until 1965 when the forest service awarded a bid to the Walt Disney Corporation for the construction of a gigantic ski resort. Of course, such a center needed a high-speed, modern highway blasted through the mountains to shuttle the 10,000 skiers a day who were anticipated. The plan sparked heated opposition by conservationists. Cartoons appeared of a giant Mickey Mouse stomping through the woods with a shovel, chasing away Bambi and her friends. The battle lasted 13 years and finally reached Congress. The pocket of Mineral King was at last attached to Sequoia National Park, but had become a well-known spot. Mineral King is slated to remain relatively isolated, accessible to those who really want to get there. One drive-in campground is available at Cold Springs.

Just south of the park on Route 198 is the town of **Three Rivers**, with the usual array of rustic motels, private campgrounds and restaurants. For down-home filling meals starting at $4.50, try the *Noisy Water Cafe*, 41775 Sierra Drive, on the north side of the road.

# Mount Whitney

Access to Mt. Whitney, the highest point in the contiguous United States at about 15,000 feet (5,100 m), is accessible for hiking and viewing from the east side of the park. The turn-off for Mt. Whitney is at **Lone Pine**, on Route 395 (also serving as the junction for the approach to Death Valley, the lowest point in the U.S., 90 miles (144 km) to the east). Mt. Whitney is the most frequently climbed peak in the Sierra Nevada, if not in the U.S. The 10.7 mile (17 km) trail begins at the **Whitney Portal** trailhead, which is 13 miles (20 km) west of Lone Pine. The road is usually open from May to early November.

This trail can be strenuous, especially to those not acclimated to high altitude, and altitude sickness can be a problem. Patches of snow can remain on the upper section of the trail all year long.

Summer days can be quite warm at the lower elevations, but temperatures at the summit are cool, and even on summer nights, temperatures often drop to freezing or below. Afternoon thunderstorms are common. Prepare for a bit of winter and summer: sunglasses, sunscreen, a brimmed hat and mosquito repellent, as well as raingear and warm clothes.

If you have some hiking experience, give it a try for some spectacular views. A 89-year old woman did it although when she tried again at age 90, she had to stop just short of the summit. Commercial shuttle service to the Whitney trailhead is available at Lone Pine from **Eastern Sierra Shuttle**: tel. 619-876-4435. For more information on climbing Whitney, call or write the Mt. Whitney Ranger District, P.O. Box 8, Lone Pine, 93545, tel. 619-876-5542.

## The Los Angeles "Water War"

The dry, sparsely populated, Owens Valley east of the Sierra is the arena for a dramatic, heated and enduring conflict. The runoff from the heavy Sierra snows was once enough to make the Owens Valley rich farm land, and to replenish the waters of Mono Lake. In 1904, however, engineers in Los Angeles realized that, with additional water, the population and economy of L.A. might boom. The best place to acquire this water, they concluded, was in Owens Valley. Many Owens Valley farmers turned a quick profit by selling acreage at inflated prices to the City of Los Angeles. Soon Los Angeles owned most of the valley, and built an aqueduct, which opened in 1913.

L.A. civic leaders who had promoted the aqueduct and knew when the water was coming and where, bought worthless land cheaply in the San Fernando valley and sold it at immense profits when the faucets were opened. Meanwhile, Owens Valley farms were squeezed dry of water, the agricultural industry collapsed, and farmers and ranchers were forced off the land either by its new owner or the lack of water. The area became a semi-desert controlled by far-away interests.

At last the locals rebelled with dynamite and for several years during the 1920s an intermittent campaign of sabotage was waged against the aqueduct system. Armed guards patrolled the channel and machine guns were mounted at strategic points. For all the fever caused by the discovery of gold in the previous century, water was showing itself as the truly precious commodity in California.

L.A. expanded further north to Mono Lake. In 1970 the city opened a second aqueduct and began pumping groundwater from the Owens Valley. Green pasturage turned into scrub desert almost overnight. The fight began again, but this time with lawsuits. Litigation came to a standstill in 1984. A compromise management plan is still being worked out.

The Owens Valley water conflict carries implications for the whole state of California. As time passes and the population grows, water resources grow more and more precious. The Owens Valley was just the beginning. Since then Los Angeles has grown at a tremendous pace and stretched its pipes north toward San Francisco and east to the Colorado River and Arizona.

How long and to what extent can one region continue its unbridled expansion and its gain, absorbing the precious resources of another region? Sixty years after the first dynamite blast along the aqueduct to Los Angeles, that question has not yet been answered, but has only become more critical.

### Accommodations

Most private lodging in both parks is managed by Guest Services,

Inc. The various lodges are somewhat over-priced. The rustic cabins are affordable, at about $20 per person. They range from bland to comfortable and pretty. Lodge and motel rooms are much more expensive. Guest services operate the lodges at Grant Grove and Cedar Grove, as well as at the *Stony Creek Lodge* between the national parks and the *Giant Forest Lodge*. Reservations are recommended for all lodges. One central office handles reservations for all these lodges: Guest Services, Inc., Reservations Dept. P.O. Box 789, Three Rivers, CA 93271, tel. 209-561-3314.

For cabins in the Mineral King area, write: *Silver City Store*, Three Rivers, CA 93271. Tel. 561-3223.

The Wilsonia Lodge, at Grant Grove, operates motel-type accommodation. For reservations, tel. 335-2310.

Campgrounds in the national parks are run by the National Park Service. Only **Lodgepole** accepts *Ticketron* reservations during the summer. The rest are strictly first-come-first-serve. The two parks have almost 15 campgrounds between them along the main routes, and it is generally possible to find a place in one of them, except on major holidays. Cost ranges from $4-$6. Any Visitor Center will offer advice on campgrounds. At Redwood Canyon it is possible to walk and sleep near the sequoias. At the campgrounds near Cedar Grove, at the end of the road, there is a sense of seclusion.

For backcountry hiking and camping, obtain a free permit first from any Visitor Center or ranger station. There are quotas for the various trails and campsites, and sometimes in summer these can fill up. However, if you are willing to be flexible, the ranger can direct you towards an unfilled alternative route. For those who are geared up for it, there is a vast amount of backcountry in both these parks to explore.

## Food

Coffee shops and restaurants are found at Cedar Grove, Grant Grove, Lodgepole and Giant Forest. While bound to be overpriced, some are not so bad. If planning to camp, however, or even just picnic, it is advisable to stock up on supplies somewhere in the valley where prices are cheaper and selection greater.

## Important addresses and phone numbers
Area Code: 209.
24-hour information recording: tel. 565-3351.
Backpacking Information: tel. 565-3307.

### Kings Canyon
Grant Grove Visitor Center: Located in Grant Grove Village, tel. 335-2315. 8am-5pm.

Cedar Grove Ranger Station: Located a quarter mile west of Cedar Grove Village, tel. 565-3341, ext. 430. 8am-5pm.

**Sequoia**
Lodgepole Visitor Center: tel. 565-3341, ext. 631. 8am-5pm.
Giant Forest Village Information Booth: tel. 561-3314. 10am-4pm through September 7th.
Ash Mountain Visitor Center: tel. 565-3456. 8am-5pm.

# Santa Barbara

Santa Barbara is situated on the gentle slopes between the Santa Inez Mountains and a westwardly arching coast. The southern orientation of its beaches and harbor and the Channel Islands temper the Pacific squalls. The deep channel supports a rich marine life, and the mountains make up a rugged, preserved wilderness area in startlingly close proximity to the city. The light here has a strange, vibrating brightness, and when the morning fog lifts, the greenery, the horizon, and the golden ridges against the blue sky stand out in sharp and brilliant relief.

Santa Barbara, in some ways, typifies the very best that southern California offers. While buffered from the urban sprawl of Los Angeles by the town of Ventura and the intervening mountains, it is by no means isolated. Santa Barbara has flash, style and urban sophistication. The University of California, at adjoining Isla Vista, adds to the cultural vibrancy and the obsession with health and recreation. Yet the tone here is casual, relaxed, friendly, and community-oriented. Santa Barbarans are deeply proud of their home and convinced that they dwell in the closest thing to earthly paradise.

The town began as a resort for the rich and almost still is. When a 1925 earthquake destroyed much of the city, residents had the vision and resources to rebuild it as a planned community while preserving the old Spanish influence. The restoration was meticulous and the character of the central district has been preserved to this day. The commercial center around State st. has been reshaped into one unified adobe aisle with tiled edgings plazas and fountains. Nothing is out of place or abrasive here. The vegetation is lush, even if it is pruned and trimmed. There are strict controls on such intrusions as billboards. Local residents fought persistently and successfully to keep Route 101 a regular thoroughfare rather than to build an obtrusive freeway (resulting today, ironically, in congested traffic).

Wealth and urbanity still flow here from Los Angeles. Young successful professionals live here and commute to the metropolis 90 minutes away. Personalities from the art and movie worlds take refuge here, as does Ronald Reagan.

Cynics refer to the place as Santa Boutique, but the gem has another facet which you can glimpse on the manicured lawns of the majestic Spanish buildings, where the homeless catch some sleep. On a summer evenings many people, from all walks of life, congregate around the railroad tracks, or in one of the public buildings or churches, for shelter for the night.

There are lots of things in Santa Barbara to keep the visitor busy. Many sites and attractions are free or nominal in cost. There are many restaurants to suit everyone's budget. Lodgings tend to be a little over-priced, but here too there is a great choice.

## How to get there

**By air:** Santa Barbara has its own airport, about eight miles (3 km) from downtown, where several state and regional carriers land, in addition to *American Airlines* and *United Airlines*. There is also a direct bus service from the Los Angeles Airport.

**By land:** The drive to Santa Barbara from Los Angeles is easy using the 101 freeway, but the traffic can snag in Santa Barbara itself. The Pacific Coast Highway is slower, but passes through some small, scenic beach towns. From the north, the main approach is again the 101 freeway. From Las Cruces in the north to Santa Barbara, Routes 1 and 101 have merged into one freeway.

**Buses:** *Amtrak*, *Greyhound* and the *Green Tortoise* (the alternative bus company) serve the city.

## In-town transportation

The *Santa Barbara Metropolitan Transit District* provides excellent bus service. A convenient map and riding guide, with major tourist sites is available from the Chamber of Commerce. The **Transit Center**, on Chapala st. at the *Greyhound* terminal, also distributes the guide. It is also the transfer point for many bus routes. Fares are 50 cents and you need the exact change to buy a ticket. Transfers are free. On weekdays during morning and evening rush hours, as well as lunchtime, free shuttlebuses run downtown along several routes at ten minute intervals. Details are available at the Transit Center or by phone.

The *Santa Barbara Trolley Company*, a private service, runs on regular scheduled routes between major hotels, tourist areas and downtown. Fare is $1, and schedules are available from the Chamber of Commerce or company offices.

Cycling is easy along the flat areas or gentle hills. Many streets have special bike lanes, if you drive be aware of cyclists.

## Food

Restaurants ranging from Mexican to Thai to good old burgers, as diverse in price as in menu, are concentrated downtown. There is a place for every taste, whim and budget. Very near downtown, a wide selection of ethnic restaurants line De La Vina st. between Calle Laurelles and Alamar. There are some fine bargains along here, especially for lunch.

The harbor area features some elaborate seafood restaurants, while

Isla Vista obviously caters to students with many reasonable pizza and felafel stands, and lunch specials.

*Joe's of Santa Barbara*: 534 State st., tel. 966-4638, is a local landmark and favorite watering hole, boasting and indeed serving the biggest drinks in town, and full hearty meals.

*Lotus Thai*: 2706 De La Vina, tel. 687-0958. What that woman creates in the tiny kitchen is remarkable. Great luncheon specials, 11am-3pm, $3 up. Dinner 5pm-10pm. A real find.

*Skandi Buffet*: 2911 De La Vina, tel. 682-3141. After you have jogged, swum and windsurfed for the day, come here. All you can eat from a terrific selection of Scandinavian food. Lunch from $3.75, 11am-4pm. Dinner from $5.50, between 4pm-8:30pm.

## Accommodations

Santa Barbara started as a resort town and still has some elegant and exclusive resorts. But now the area is accessible to almost everyone, and on a summer weekend, it seems that almost everyone is there. Reservations are required at many lodgings and are recommended all year round to avoid problems. Some establishments lower their prices in winter by as much as 30%.

Groups of standard motels and hotels can be found along Cabrillo, near the beaches, and on State st. inland from the commercial center. B&B inns tend to be scattered around, some right in downtown, some in sedate residential neighbourhoods. They run in the same range as many standard motels. Most standard motel rooms, with the exception of *Motel 6*, start at $30-$35 a night. The cheaper old residential hotels are in the bad part of town.

There are several centralized clearinghouses for vacation lodgings, at no cost to the visitor. They will give you a wide range of detailed information.

*Accommodations in Santa Barbara*: 1216 State st., SB 93101, tel. 963-9518. Centralized reservations service, for hotels, motels, B&B. No charge.

*D.B. Tourist Co.*: tel 687-8605. Reservations clearinghouse. No charge.

*Executive Houses of Santa Barbara*: 205 E. Carrillo, SB 93101, tel. 963-9350. Reservation service for weekend, weekly and monthly rentals in condos and houses.

### Expensive

*Ambassador by the Sea*, 202 W. Cabrillo blvd., 93101, tel. 965-4577. Great location near Stearns Wharf. Good place for sun worshipers.

*Brinkerhoff Inn*: 523 Brinkerhoff ave., SB 93101, tel. 963-7844; toll-free in state, 800-BEST-BNB. An old Victorian home in a district marked by Victorian landmarks and antique stores. Small and homey, continental breakfast.

*Villa Motel:* 3885 State st., SB 93105, tel. 687-3217. Away from downtown.

**Inexpensive**
*Motel 6:* 443 Corona del Mar, tel. 564-1392. Near the beach. Or 3505 State st., tel 687-5400. Beyond downtown. Reservations at both highly recommended.

**Camping**
Camping sites are plentiful in the general Santa Barbara vicinity, but there are few immediately adjacent to the city. The coastal state park campsites are right off the highway and become Winnebago City at night. They all require reservations, except Gaviota State Park, which is 32 miles (51 km) northwest of Santa Barbara and a little bit off the highway.

Santa Barbara County also operates several campgrounds, in the Lake Cachuma region and along the beach. The Jalame Beach campground, about 40 miles (64 km) northwest of the city, is on a secluded stretch of coast near Point Conception, well off the beaten track. Follow Route 101 north to Route 1, take Route 1 to Jalama rd., towards Point Conception, and follow this road to the beach. First-come first-serve, $6 per night, tel. 734-1446.

Along the winding Route 154 which goes toward San Marcos Pass, there are a number of campgrounds in Los Padres National Forest. Some lie within access of the San Rafael Wilderness area. Fees vary with facilities, ranging from free to $5 per night. All campsites are allocated on first arrival. Check with the local Forest Service office for details, tel. 683-6711.

## Tourist sites
Santa Barbara sustains a lively and diverse cultural and entertainment world. Galleries, clubs, theaters and museums thrive here.

*The Weekly* and the *Visitor Press* are two free papers which list weekly cultural events. They can be found in stores and restaurants throughout the city. The Chamber of Commerce also publishes updated information on what's happening.

The *Arts and Lectures* program of the University of California sponsors student productions, as well as visiting performers. For information on events, tel. 961-3535.

Isla Vista, the student neighborhood near the university, offers rowdy bars with live music.

If you visit in early August you will have the good fortune to be in time for the **Old Spanish Days Fiesta**. Modeled after the old Spanish harvest festivals, this is not a trivial county fair with tortillas replacing burgers. For a week the town goes crazy for

## *DOWNTOWN SANTA BARBARA*

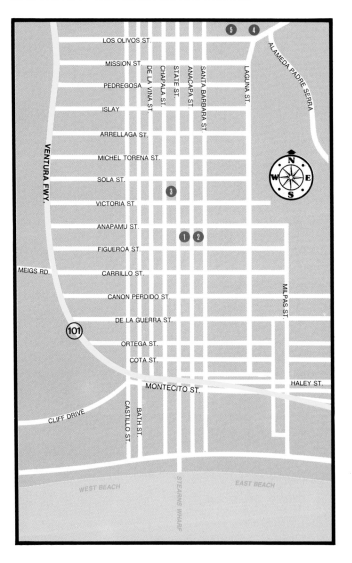

**Index**

1. Art Museum
2. Court Museum
3. Arlington Theater
4. The Mission
5. Historical Museum

everything Spanish. Office workers are released early and the bars are packed day and night. There are free events in the plazas, dancing in the courthouse courtyard, parades with fancy floats and street performers everywhere. The festival draws world-renowned performers, such as guitar virtuoso Carlos Montoya. Some events cost money, but you can be easily and endlessly entertained without spending a dime. Just bring your camera, appetite and dancing shoes. Make your room reservations well in advance. The schedule of events is available from the Chamber of Commerce.

## State st.

State st., between De La Guerra and Anapamu, is the heart of the renovated commercial district and has a concentration of beautiful public buildings. The adobe fronts, red tile roofs, wrought-iron filligree and semi-tropical gardens are everywhere. You can pick up a map at the Chamber of Commerce for a self-guiding tour.

At the heart of State st. is the **Santa Barbara Museum of Art**, a real treasure house. 1130 State st. Tues.-Sat. 11am-5pm, Thurs. 11am-9pm, Sun. noon-5pm, tel. 963-4364. Though a small museum, it attracts some of the finest exhibits touring the country. Its own collection includes classical antiquities and the works of the Renaissance painters, the French Impressionists and American moderns. Photography receives a strong emphasis. There is a concert every Sunday at 2:30pm, lectures every Thursday at 7:30pm, and a regular schedule of special events.

The museum is connected by a grassy plaza to the **public library**, which fits into the Spanish motif and makes a soothing spot to escape the eternally bright sun and rest your weary feet.

Also near the museum is **El Paseo**, a shopping arcade with stone sidewalks, Spanish tiles and a fountain. Across the street, at the Plaza De La Guerra, is the site where the first city council met in 1850.

The **Arlington Theater** is an old 1930s movie palace at 1317 State st., tel. 966-4566. It is ornate, lavish and conspicuous, and features a continuously changing program ranging from drama to rock, and classical music to classic films. The murals above the entrance depict scenes from old Mexican California and are worth viewing even if you do not see the show.

**The County Courthouse**, 1100 Anacapa st., is a dazzling architectural puzzle not to be missed. The winding staircases, Tunisian tile patterns, turrets, towers, and off-center arches — all somehow fit to create a delightful asymmetry.

Do not miss the historical murals inside. An elevator will take you up to **El Mirador**, the 70-foot (24 m) observation and clock tower from which you can see Santa Barbara spread out beneath you. Open 8am-5pm weekdays, 9am-5pm weekends and holidays. Free guided tours each Friday at 10:30am, tel. 962-6464.

**Beyond State st.**

**The Santa Barbara Mission**, completed in 1786, was the 10th in a chain of Franciscan missions in California. Referred to today as the "Queen of the missions", it is a massive and imposing white adobe building with two towers, offset by lush greenery both outside and within its courtyard.

An elaborate aqueduct, built by the local converted Indians, channeled water from mountain creeks to the mission's extensive landholdings, which grew grains, vegetables, olive trees and grape vines. The **Mission Museum** reconstructs the padres' workshops, kitchens and sleeping quarters, vividly depicting the rustic and simple mission life. Laguna st. near Mission st. Open daily 9am-5pm, Sun. 1pm-5pm, admission costs $1, children admitted free, tel. 682-4713.

The site of the dam built by Indians for mission lands is part of the **Santa Barbara Botanical Gardens**, just north of the mission at 1212 Mission Canyon rd. Open daily 8am-sunset. Guided tour on Thurs. at 10:30am and Sun. at 11am. Admission free, tel. 682-4726. Three miles (5 km) of nature trails weave through stands of cacti, wildflowers and other native plants, that are arranged by ecological zone.

**The Santa Barbara Museum of Natural History** displays the rich environmental and biological diversity of the Pacific coast, in a graceful Spanish building at 2559 Puesta del Sol rd. two blocks north of the mission. Open Mon.-Sat. 9am-5pm, Sun. and holidays 10am-5pm. Admission charged, tel. 682-4711. The museum also organizes trips, including expeditions to the Channel Islands.

The **Santa Barbara Historical Museum** is housed in an adobe building at 136 East de la Guerra st. Open Tues.-Fri. noon-5pm, Sat-Sun. 1-5pm. tel. 966-1601. The museum covers the major periods in local development, with an emphasis is on Mexican and Spanish history.

Santa Barbara is a haven for antique collectors or browsers. There are almost a hundred shops in the area, with a sizable cluster along **Brinkerhoff ave.**, off Haley between Chapala and De La Vina sts., not far from downtown.

Santa Barbara's harbor has, like many others, found tourism increasingly profitable, while the traditional activity of commercial fishing struggles along. There are as many pleasure boats in the channel as there are fishing vessels, but at twilight you can still watch the fishing boats haul in catches of shark, halibut, sole and shrimp. Tourist shops and seafood restaurants line **Stearns Wharf**. Steamed lobster or crab can be bought and eaten on the spot. The wharf is lined with anglers and you don't need a license to join them. The **Stearns Wharf Winery**, with its open deck, is a fine place to indulge in a little wine-tasting. Amid the more commercial storefronts is the **Santa Cruz Island Project Visitor Center** of the non-profit **Nature Conservancy**, with video and photographic exhibits and information on the Channel Islands. Open 11am-2pm daily.

A refreshing shoreline route for walking, jogging or cycling runs from Leadbetter Beach, just west of The Breakwater, past West Beach near Stearns Wharf, to East Beach near the Andree Clark Bird Refuge. If you still have some excess energy, the **Cabrillo Bathhouse Pavilion** on East Beach has a new weight room and beach volley ball courts at 1118 E Cabrillo blvd. Open 8am-7pm, tel. 965-0509. Open to the public, the weight room, lockers and showers cost $1.50 per day.

Parking at Stearns Wharf can get crowded and costs $1 per hr, although it's free if validated with a $3 purchase. At the foot of the wharf or in the harbor lot, parking is 50 cents per hour. On Cabrillo there is free 90-minute and all-day parking.

The Santa Barbara Harbor is the place for water sports: boating, diving, fishing, surfing, windsurfing, bodysurfing and body-watching. Rentals and lessons for windsurfing, scuba diving and sailing are available from various outfits on Stearns Wharf and the Breakwater.

At the end of East Beach are the **Santa Barbara Zoological Gardens** and the adjoining **Andree Clark Bird Refuge**. Open 10am-5pm daily. Admission charged, discounts for children, teenagers and seniors, tel. 962-6310. The zoo is small but a lot of fun for kids. The bird refuge, set around a lagoon, has paths for walking and cycling and is delightful. You can pick up a pamphlet on birds at the Natural History Museum to bring with you here.

Craftsmen and artisans from the region spread their wares out along Palm Park in a weekly bazaar every Sunday from 10am-sunset.

On Chapala st. near the foot of State st., the immense **Moreton Bay Fig Tree**, a Santa Barbara feature by now, casts shade upon locals and visitors. Transplanted in 1877 from Australia, the tree became a local *cause celebre* when it was threatened with destruction to make room for a gas station.

## Near Santa Barbara

Northwest of Santa Barbara, Route 1 splits off from Highway 101 and become a small country road leading towards the coast. It might be preferable to take the faster inland route here. Little of the shoreline is easily accessible in this area, and there is a more interesting detour to the east.

If heading north from Santa Barbara, follow Route 154 rather than Route 101. This will link up with 101 again at Beullton. But first the road winds into the rugged, scrubby Santa Inez Mountains, and over the San Marcos Pass, from which you can see the Channel Islands. There is rugged hiking in the **San Rafael Wilderness** (part of the Los Padres National Forest) and this road provides the closest access. Further along, Lake Cachuma — a popular recreation area — spreads to the right. The public campgrounds here fill up fast.

A little further along Route 154 is the junction with Route 246 which heads west, to the town of **Solvang**. Settled in 1911 by Danish-Americans, the town was small and obscure until after World War II. Now it has been rediscovered, restored and sugar-coated, and its original quaintness has been lost — but there is no doubt about the scrumptiousness of its pastries.

Nearby **Mission on Santa Ines**, built in 1804 as 19th in the mission chain, was largely destroyed over time. The chapel appears as it did in the early days. The tour-by-loudspeaker leaves a bit to be desired.

The Santa Inez Valley has seen a resurgence of the wine industry. The Solvang Chamber of Commerce can supply details on wineries which offer wine tastings.

Follow 254 back to the 101 highway, at Beullton, and at the junction you'll find *Anderson's*, justly famous for its pea soup.


# Channel Islands National Park

Five of the eight islands in the Channel Island chain, off the Santa Barbara coast, comprise the **Channel Islands National Park**. Isolation from the mainland, the mingling of warm and cold water currents in the deep channel, and exposure to the harsh Pacific elements, have created unique and delicately balanced ecological zones here. They differ as sharply from each other as they do from the mainland ecology. Many organisms and communities, highly specialized, belong to both land and sea, and any change in either environment has far-reaching effects.

Seafaring Chumash Indians lived on these islands for thousands of years. When explorer Juan Rodriguez Cabrillo explored the coast on behalf of Spain, he found about 2,000 Indians living on one island alone. Cabrillo himself, credited with the first exploration of the California coast, died here after a fall, probably on San Miguel Island. He is thought to be buried there but his grave remains undiscovered. By the end of the 18th century, hunters, settlers and ranchers had reached the islands, and in the following decades the Indians were removed to the mainland mission at Santa Barbara. Seals and sea otters were hunted almost to extinction. Grazing animals and foreign plant species upset the fragile ecological balance and threatened or totally erased some rare and singular species. Only recently were some of the islands preserved, and the immediate marine region around them was declared a National Marine Sanctuary. The rules controlling the visits and effects of humans are strict and rigourously enforced, with the intent of restoring the previous natural balance.

Four of the islands can be visited. **Santa Cruz Island**, the largest, is currently in private hands. Only specific sections can be visited, in organized trips arranged by the private concessionaires, Island Packers, or the non-profit Nature Conservancy. **Anacapa Island**, the smallest, is actually a chain of three small islands. Near the National Park Visitors Center on the eastern island begins a self-guiding nature trail 1.5 (2.4 km) miles long. Guided walks and evening programs are available.

**Santa Barbara Island**, the southernmost in the chain, is an excellent spot for observing sea lions and elephant seals, especially during the winter when they breed on the island. On San Miguel, the westernmost and most exposed, the Pacific forces have sculpted a harsh and starkly beautiful landscape. A 15-mile (24-km) round-trip-trail for the hardy follows the length of the island.

Anacapa and Santa Barbara Islands have primitive campgrounds, each for about 30 people. For those who enjoyed the adventures of Robinson Crusoe, obtain a permit in advance from park headquarters and bring everything you need with you, as no supplies are available.

The mainland **National Park Visitor Center** in Ventura (1901 Spinnaker dr., tel. 664-8262), offers a 25-minute film on the park, as well as displays of tidepools, native plants and Chumash artifacts. Pick up brochures, maps and camping permits here.

Immediately next door, 1867 Spinnaker dr., Ventura, tel. 642-1393, in the parking lot, is the office of Island Packers, the main concessionaire operating Channel Island expeditions. The full spring and summer schedule is curtailed after August. Reservations are advisable. Rates start, depending on the trip, from about $25 per person.

The Santa Barbara Museum of Natural History leads trips to Santa Cruz and San Miguel Islands, tel. 962-9111.

## Important addresses and phone numbers

Santa Barbara Chamber of Commerce: 1330 State st., tel. 965-3021.
Solvang Chamber of Commerce: 1623 Mission dr., tel. 688-3317.
Airport: 515 Marxmiller rd., Goleta, tel. 967-5608.
Airport Express: tel. 965-1611. Service to and from Santa Barbara Airport.
*Santa Barbara Airbus*: tel. 964-7374. To and from L.A. Airport.
*Santa Barbara Metropolitan Transit District*: Carrillo and Chapala sts., tel 683-3702.
*Santa Barbara Trolley Co.*: 125 Harbor Way, tel. 962-0209.
*Amtrak*: 209 State st., tel. 687-6848.
*Greyhound*: Carrillo and Chapala, tel. 966-3962.

# CALIFORNIA

*Green Tortoise*: tel. 569-1884.
U.S. Forest Service: 6144 Calle Real, Goleta, tel. 683-6711.
Crisis Hotline: tel. 964-6713.
Area code: tel. 805.

# San Luis Obispo

San Luis Obispo nestles in a small valley between the Santa Lucia mountains and some gorgeous beaches. By no means a metropolis, it is nevertheless the largest city in the region, and the region's cattle and dairy center. To the north, the inland valleys embrace rich wine country. Along the coast to the northwest, small towns are sparsely strung. There is something very elusive about the beauty of these coastal hills.

Downtown San Luis Obispo invites a stroll. It still has a friendly small-town atmosphere. You will find J.C. Penny's and French bakeries, junk shops and outdoor cafes, galleries showing the work of local craftsmen, and ornate, well preserved Victorian architecture.

## How to get there

From San Luis Obispo south, Routes 101 and 1 converge; heading north, they split, to join again near Monterey. To the north, 101 follows the inland valleys through dairyland and the Pas Robles wine country. Route 1 continues along the cliffs of Big Sur.

San Louis Obispo lies on the coastal *Amtrak* route. The ride by train is slower and slightly more expensive than by bus, but is relaxing and has beautiful views as it skirts the coastline. The buses run inland.

Four basic bus routes serve the town and its outskirts. The City Hall at Osos and Palm is the transfer for all buses, which operate on a half-hourly basis. Although there are marked bus stops, you can, in true small-town spirit, flag down a bus at any corner. Buses stop running at 7pm. Tickets 50 cents, transfers free. A monthly pass costs $16, and only $2.50 for seniors. Special service for the handicapped. *SLOCAT* (SLO County Area Transit) buses serve the coastal towns up to San Simeon. It runs a full weekday schedule, with curtailed service on Saturday and none on Sunday. Tickets from 25 cents to $1.

## Accommodations

If budget is your main consideration, then the most appropriate lodging will be found inland, near San Luis Obispo, rather than in the coastal towns. There are numerous motels and hotels to choose from along the coast, ranging from about $34 and up. The strip of motels and hotels in San Simeon, along Castillo dr., bordering the highway, tends to be a bit more expensive than those further

## *SAN LUIS OBISPO*

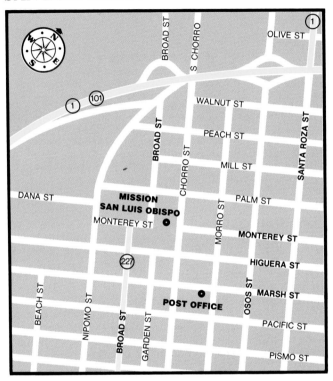

south, as this is the last stop for those heading north, south of Big Sur.

As with many regions some of the B&Bs are in the same price range as motels. On this coast expecially, some of the houses are very charming.

### Expensive
*Madonna Inn*: 100 Madonna rd., San Luis Obispo. Each room a bizarre, separate world. Go for the room in bubble gum pink. It is worth the stop just to look around, tel. 543-3000.

### Moderate
*Silver Surf Motel*: 9390 Castillo dr., San Simeon. Near the ocean. Jacuzzi and pool. The *Hearst Castle Special* includes 3 days/2 nights, Tour 1 tickets, one dinner and one breakfast for two people. $55 per person, tel. 927-4661.

*Heritage Inn B&B*: 978 Olive st. $44-$73. Low winter, mid-week rates. A small restored Victorian building, with home-made breakfasts, tel. 544-7440.

### Inexpensive
*Blue Bell Motel*: 3053 S. Higuera st. Standard, clean and cheap. (slightly more on weekends and holidays), tel. 543-6807.
*Megan's Friends B&B referrals*: 1776 Royal Way, San Luis Obispo 93401, tel. 544-4406. Listings available by phone or mail.

**Camping facilities** are available at most of the state parks from Pismo Beach to San Simeon. Some are filled with trailers and dune buggies. **Montana De Oro State Park** is outstanding, situated in a deep and quiet valley, with 50 primitive sites plus some well developed sites too. Seven miles (11 km) south of Los Osos on Pecho rd., tel. 772-2560.

## Food

*Chuckwagon Restaurant*: Route 1 and Moonstone Beach dr., Cambria. All you can eat of fine meat entrees and salad bar.
*Apple Farm Restaurant*: 2015 Monterey. Home-made soups and pies. Good salad bar, homey atmosphere. Moderate.
*The Bakery Cafe*: 1040 Broad st. Croissants and expresso alongside the creek in the heart of town.
*Budget Cafe*: 1216 Archer st. It's friendly and serves filling and inexpensive dishes for $5 or less.
*Cafe Roma*: 1819 Osos st. Behind an old storefront, serving home-made pasta which is made fresh each day, and delicious fish. Friendly and moderately priced.

## Tourist sites

The visitor center in downtown SLO provides a brochure for a self-guided tour of downtown, highlighting the old Victorian architecture. More interesting, however, than an old gabled Victorian building is the ceiling of the **Fremont Theater** on Santa Rosa st. near Monterey st. This Art Deco gem features sea nymphs riding stallions across the ceiling.

Near the visitors center is **Mission Plaza**, in Chorro st. Open in summer 9am-5pm, winter 10am-4pm. Donation requested, tel. 543-8562.

The adjacent mission was the first building in the area, founded by Junipero Serra in 1772 as the fifth mission in his chain. As in many cases, the town developed around the mission. This mission was the first to construct the famous red-tile roof, for defense against firebrands shot by Indians. The mission is still used today and houses a museum with some relics, photos and prints of its history.

The plaza is the center of downtown. San Luis Creek, which supplied the early mission with water, runs past. There are one or two nice cafes on its banks, surrounded by thick vegetation. It's a nice place to absorb the sun, the colors and the street music. The plaza is the focus for most festivals, both formal and spontaneous. In February there is a Mardi Gras, in spring a Spanish Fiesta, in August a well-known Mozart Festival and in September a wine-tasting festival.

The **City Historical Museum**, 696 Monterey st. Open Wed.-Sun. 10am-4pm. Admission free, tel. 543-0638, across from the mission, has a small collection of artifacts, including the sombrero of Pio Pico, the last Spanish governor of California. The employees are proud of their town and seem to know all the interesting excursions and side roads.

Two downtown mini-malls are housed in old buildings. **The Network**, on Higuera st., was an early department store, and **The Creamery**, on Nipomo, was in fact a creamery. The **SLO Art Center** on Monterey st. near the plaza highlights some beautiful work by local artists. Open Tues.-Sun. noon-5pm.

**California Polytechnic Institute** (Cal Poly in local jargon), located just north of downtown, maintains a huge working farm and extensive research facilities for agricultural subjects. The school brings an influx of young people and money to town. It also holds an amazing annual rodeo as part of the **Poly Royal** fair in late April. Tours of the farm and facilities are available, and the achievements of the school may well renew one's faith in the green revolution. Parking permits at the administration building. Information desk, tel. 546-0111.

The famous **Madonna Inn**, just south of town on Highway 101, reaches new heights of fantastical architecture, decor and the plugged-in gingerbread effect. Even Alice and the Cheshire Cat would be baffled here. For lodging details see below.

Wineries and vineyards are clustered around the Paso Robles-Templeton area along Route 101. York Mountain Road offers a winding scenic trip across the mountains between the two main highways. There are several excellent wineries along this road, including the **York Mountain Winery**, oldest in the region. Open daily for tasting 10am-5pm. It dates back to 1882, with its ivy covered tasting room and rock walls dug into the hillside. A list of regional wineries is available at the SLO visitor center or the Paso Robles Chamber of Commerce.

**Mission San Miguel**, near 101 about eight miles north of Paso Robles, is one of the most authentic of the missions. It has not been excessively spruced up and the buildings are stark.

The frescoes inside are bright, and there must be some fascinating untold dramas behind them, for they were executed by unknown Indian painters under mission direction. Take the mission exit in

San Miguel. Open during daylight hours, tours from 10am-5pm, tel. 467-3256.

The beach towns to the south of SLO — **Avila**, **Shell Beach** and **Pismo** — tend to be overcrowded. Avila has been overrun by waves of teenagers, and the southern part of the Pismo sands have been invaded by dune buggies. However, seven miles (11 km) south of **Los Osos** is the quiet secluded **Montana de Oro State Park**, with abundant wildlife, great beachcombing at Spooner's Cove beach, and good camping (see below).

Northwest of San Louis Obispo, on Route 1, is the resort and fishing village of **Morro Bay**, which took its name from **Morro Rock**, a huge rock rising 600 feet (204 m) from the water. One of a chain of nine extinct volcanic cones, the rock was named by the explorer Juan Cabrillo in 1542 because it resembles the turbans worn by the Spanish Moors. It can be reached by a causeway from the beach area north of town.

South of the town, **Morro Bay State Park** contains one of the outstanding marine life zones on the central coast, with the habitats of a lagoon and natural bay. There are great spots for surf fishing, clamming or just exploring among the rocks and driftwood. The *Clam Taxi*, which operates all year round, runs from the Morro Bay Marino at 4th st. to the park.

The **Natural History Museum**, open daily 10am-5pm, tel. 772-2560, facing across the bay, covers Chumash Indian life, local geology and oceanography. There are nature walks and ranger programs.

Various types of fish, as well as abalone and oysters, comprise the local hauls and can be bought fresh at the fish markets found along the embarcadero. Otherwise, try them at one of the seafood restaurants which prepare early bird specials.

If you want to go fishing yourself, you can do it without a license at the public T-pier. There are several sportfishing outfits along the embarcadero that run cruises ranging from half-day to two days. They cost about $20 for a full day. Pole and tackle are extra. The **Morro Bay Marina**, 699 Embarcadero. Open daily 9am-4:30pm, tel. 772-8085, rents small motorboats for forays into the bay, at $10 per hour.

North of Morro Bay and Cayuco, on Route 1, is the town of **Harmony** with a population of about 20, depending on the day. Everyone in this transformed dairy town is some kind of artist or craftsman. On summer Sunday afternoons from 2pm-5pm you can catch an outdoor jazz, ragtime or bluegrass concert.

**Cambria**, north of Harmony, is another town with many artisans, especially along Burton Drive in the East Village. Moonstone Beach Drive winds along the coast past galleries, restaurants, and the Sea Otter Refuge at **Leffingwell's Landing**.

*Heasrt Castle*

**The Hearst San Simeon State Historical Monument** — or Hearst's Castle — is undoubtedly the outstanding tourist site along the coast south of Big Sur. It is a overwhelming, flamboyant baronial 20th-century dreamland, known by its owner as "the ranch".

The land was indeed first acquired as a ranch by George Hearst. William Randolf, his only son, built a newspaper empire based on inflammatory "yellow journalism", which helped ignite the Spanish-American War in 1898. Before the outbreak of the war, he is reported to have said to his illustrator in Cuba: "You provide the pictures and I'll provide the war".

When the family ranch fell to him, he spared no expense in indulging his whims and fantasies. The main building, on a hilltop in the Santa Lucias with views along the coast, boasts over a hundred rooms. Steel, cement, top soil, plants, as well as the dismantled furnishings, walls, and rooms of European estates, were shipped by steamer to the San Simeon port and hauled up the winding road. The grounds and other buildings present a dizzying clash and blend of styles ranging from Roman to Gothic to Moorish.

Medieval hangings, Chinese ceramics and other priceless antiques were flown in from around the world. The library holds the world's largest private collection of Greek vases. And yet, puzzlingly, the mansion holds a large number of cheap plaster copies as well.

Hearst's lavishness extended to the surrounding countryside, which he filled with herds of zebra, white deer and other exotic species. His private zoo held monkeys, cheetahs and lions.

The impetus for much of this frenetic construction was the creation of a hideway for his Hollywood movie queen, Marion Davies. Movie stars came up for Hearst's feasts, and other guests included Winston Churchill and President Calvin Coolidge.

There was, however, something strange and lonely in all this extravagance, a feeling best captured by Orson Welles' cinematic masterpiece, *Citizen Kane*, which is worth seeing, if possible, before a visit to the estate.

The area deeded to the state is but a small portion of the land holdings which still belong to the Hearst family, and which encompass most of the town and beachfront below.

Visits to the castle are by guided tour only. There are three different tours which operate throughout the year, and a fourth from April to Oct. Each tour involves a fair amount of walking and climbing and costs $10, $5 for ages 6-12. Each lasts almost two hours. The different tours can all be done on one day, or taken on separate days. The ticket office is open from 8am-4pm daily. Tours leave at least once every hour, from 8:20am-3pm in winter, and more often during holidays and the summer.

Tickets may be bought upon entry, but reservations are recommended, particularly during the summer. For reservations made from within the state, tel. 800-444-PARK, or make them through any local *Ticketron* outlet. For information within the state, tel. 800-952-5580. From out-of-state call tel. 619-452-1950 for reservations and information. For visitors confined to wheelchairs, special arrangements can be made by calling the castle directly, tel. 927-4622.

The first tour, an overview, can accommodate about 50 people. The others are much smaller. Tours 2 and 3 explore the upper levels of the castle itself, while the 4th surveys the grounds and architecture.

## Important addresses and phone numbers

Visitor Information: 1039 Chorro st., at Higuera. Daily 8am-5pm, tel. 543-1323.
*Greyhound*: 150 South st. Open 5:45am-9:15pm, tel. 543-2121.
*Amtrak*: Railroad Ave and Santa Rosa. Reservations 9:30am-5:30pm, tel. 541-0505.
State Park Information: tel. 549-3312.

# CALIFORNIA

Paso Robles Chamber of Commerce: 1113 Spring, tel. 238-0506.
Emergency: 911.
Area Code: 805.

# Big Sur

*On rising I would go to the cabin door and, casting my eyes over the velvety, rolling hills, such a feeling of contentment, such a feeling of gratitude was mine that instinctively my hand went up in benediction.*

Henry Miller: *Big Sur and the Oranges of Hieronymus Bosch.*

Big Sur's mountains are not the highest, nor its forests the richest, nor its canyons the deepest, but there is something inexpressibly wild and beautiful in the rugged coastline between Carmel and San Simeon, shrouded in fog, engulfed by the sound of the crashing waves.

Big Sur lies in the middle of the central coast of California, an area roughly defined as extending from the San Louis Obispo region in the south to the Monterey Bay and Santa Cruz in the north. Big Sur looms in the middle as a border between the two.

From the days of the earliest settlers, Big Sur has held a strange attraction for people. Some came to cut down the redwoods or to build a navigable port; others drifted in to find a simple basic life in nature. They lived as small farmers, carpenters and the like. A few artists discovered the area and moved in. The American poet Robinson Jeffers worked as a stonecutter in these hills while steeping himself in images of "the lean redges" and "the prehuman dignity of night".

With the building of Highway 1 (much of it by convict labor) along what was once a rutted wagon trail, Big Sur was opened up to the rest of California and the world, with the predictable encroachments, developments and eager plans for profit-making resorts. Today, bits of the cliff are dotted with expensive homes. The area became a center for people who, during and after the 1960s, sought quieter, simpler lives based on crafts and independent physical labor. It has attracted many people of alternative lifestyles, therapies, cults, etc.

Today there are even fewer people living in the area — between 700 and 800 in all — than there were in the beginning of the century when there were greater efforts to exploit the local resources. The "urban" area runs through the valley paralleling the Big Sur River, set back a mile or so from the coast. It extends from the **Jules Pfeiffer State Park** and the **Big Sur Lodge**, to the north for about six miles (4 km). There are a few lodges, hotels and restaurants in the area, plus an occasional gift shop, and a few mailboxes and no-trespassing signs on some dirt roads.

# BIG SUR AREA

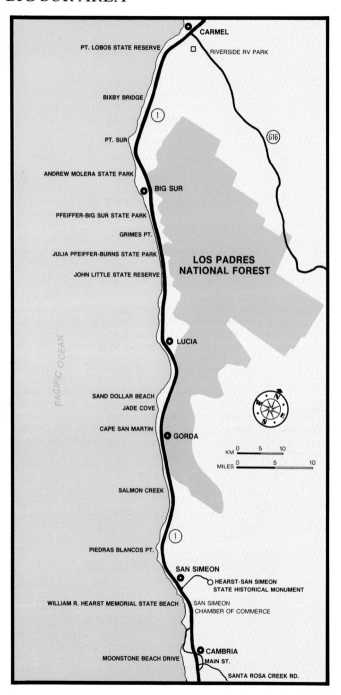

## How to get there

**By car:** The drive between San Francisco and Los Angeles, along the gorgeous coast highway, takes about 12 hours or less. At both ends of this stretch — at San Louis Obispo in the south and Monterey in the north — you can pick up Highway 101 which will bring you more rapidly to the cities. It is very difficult to reach Big Sur other than by car, organized tour, or bicycle (hitching not recommended).

**By bus:** The *Monterey Peninsula Transit System*, tel. 408-899-2555, makes two round trips daily from Carmel to the Nepenthe parking lot, daily during the summer, and weekends only during the winter. As of this writing, however, the possibility was raised that this service would be curtailed or stopped for budgetary reasons, so check first. From the south, the nearest public bus that runs to Big Sur is the *San Louis Obispo System* bus between San Simeon and Morrow Bay.

In spring, the hills are covered with flowers all the way down to the ocean. Autumn has a burnished beauty all its own. The winter brings damp, chilly mists and heavy rainfall, but rarely snow, and the greyness is often broken by gleaming, polished blue skies. The fog bank seldom crosses the coastal ridge into the interior hills and valleys, so hikers in the interior hills and valleys may find it broiling hot while the coast is cool. Avoid the Labor Day and July 4th weekends.

Facilities vary between the very elegant and expensive cliffside or hilltop restaurants and inns, to off-trail campsites. There is little in between. Everything from gasoline to beer to a cup of coffee could cost up to double the price here, so fill up the tank, cooler, and thermos. Camp out if you can, and try, whenever possible, to park your car and go hiking. There are pull-offs along the road, as well as extensive trails in the parks. Groves of redwood trees fill the deep ravines that go right down to the cliffs, and make for beautiful walks. Some paths lead down to the beach, others along the edges of sheer cliffs. (The sign that warns of danger means business.) In Big Sur you can escape the hordes of motorists the moment you pull off the highway into a hiking area.

# Public Parks and Campgrounds

Big Sur has an excellent system of parks, enabling visitors — from the casual stroller and photographer to the serious hiker — to taste the varied beauty of the area. There are enough campgrounds and enough variety to serve every kind of camper. Cyclists can stay in any state parkground for 50 cents and cannot, by law, be turned away. The different parks are listed here in geographical order, from north to south.

At the northern end of Big Sur, south of the *Rocky Point*

*Restaurant* and a few miles north of the **Point Sur Lighthouse**, Paolo Colorado Road turns to the east, toward **Botcher Campground** (Forest Service) in the hills. There is also an unnamed Forest Service campground off a dirt spur to the left, through a gate which is not always open. A drive through the lower part of the canyon is in itself beautiful, with quaint little houses nestled between the trees, like a redwood hobbitland.

Situated near the mouth of the Big Sur River, the entrance to **Andrew Molera State Park** is on the west side of the highway, but vehicles cannot pass beyond the unpaved parking lot. From there a quarter-mile long path leads to (about 50) campsites in an open meadow. The path continues through a pretty wood, and then to the floodplain formed by the river. The park faces both the shallow river and the rough ocean. It is pleasant to be away from all the trailers and highway noise. There are ten miles (16 km) of hiking trails. Campsites cost 50 cents and have a three-night limit. For information: Pfeiffer Big Sur State Park, tel. 667-2315. Adjacent to the park, **Big Sur Trail Rides** offers short guided horse rides, as well as pack trips, into the Ventana wilderness area, tel. 667-2666.

The **Pfeiffer Big Sur State Park** (not to be confused with the Julia Pfeiffer Burns State Park further south) is a highly developed park, with a lodge, cabins, a store, a restaurant and campfire programs and nature walks in summer. It is a great park for hiking, as there are many short, interlocking trails that make easy loops. There is a very short nature trail, as well as longer, tougher trails throughout the park, and trails leading into the Ventana Wilderness. Within this one park there are redwood forests, waterfalls, oak forest, high chaparral, and stunning views of the mountains and the rocky coast stretching in both directions. There is a beautiful hike to **Pfeiffer Falls** through a fern-lined canyon. The park has both campsites and trailer slots available by reservation, with a seven-day limit. For reservations write to: Department of Parks and Recreation. P.O.Box 2390, Sacramento, 95811. Contact any *Ticketron* office. Local phone: 667-2315.

Just south of the Big Sur State Park entrance is the National Forest Service information booth. The **Ventana Wilderness**, which is part of the Los Padres National Forest, covers a large area of forest and chaparral behind the Big Sur State Park. This area is isolated, and filled with wildlife. Wilderness permits (free) are required, and are available from 8am to 4:30pm at the station or in advance by calling or writing: P.O. Box 64, Big Sur, CA 93920, tel. 667-2423. Maps of Ventana Wilderness trails are available at the station.

Also administered by the Forest Service is **Pfeiffer Beach**. Turn west onto **Sycamore Canyon Road**, just a hundred yards or so south of the forest service information station, down a steep short incline that leads about one-and-a+half miles (2.5 km) to a parking lot. From there you walk. The first thing that you will notice is the

*Big Sur landscape*

large monolithic rock looming from the water like the prow of a huge ship. The beach is unusually flat and wide for the Big Sur coast, and uncrowded as well. The beach which is for day use only has spur-like cliffs at either end, and in the north it merges with the beach and hills of Andrew Molera State Park, thus providing quite a large area for beach-combing and exploration.

A little less than 10 miles (16 km) further south is the **Julia Pfeiffer Burns State Park**, a shady and peaceful day-use area situated right off the road. There's a charge for entering by car, but there is space to park outside by the road, and lots of people do this. Trails lead up through a narrow, dark and peaceful redwood grove, or under the highway to a waterfall that drops right into the ocean. Although camping is not officially allowed, there seems to be an understanding that in a certain area camping is permitted. Just outside the park entrance, only 30 yards or so to the south, is a gate on the ocean side of the road. Beyond this gate, a path curves around the cove from which the waterfall plunges. The path goes down through an open field and doubles back into a shaded grove just above a rocky promontory where the waves surge and blast as if through a tunnel. In this peaceful grove there is enough

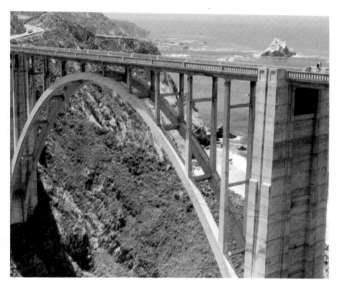

*Highway 1*

space for four or five tents, and it seems to be a locally known spot. But don't press your luck and start a fire. The rocky shore is a haunt for sea otters, and the area is, in fact, an underwater refuge as well. Threatened with extinction not long ago, the otters now survive among the thick offshore kelp beds.

Further to the south are two forest service campgrounds, the Kirk Creek Campground, tel. 805 927-4211, at the Mill Creek picnic area, and the Plasket Creek Campground, tel. 805 927-4556, near **Sand Dollar Beach** and **Jade Cove**. It is sometimes possible to find jade which has been washed up at **Jade Beach**, which is also a nude sun-bathing spot.

Several other sites are of interest: the **Esalen Institute**, named after the local Indians, has crystallized into an institute of all the various disciplines and forms of the "human potential movement" which is as uniquely Californian as the redwoods. As if selecting from a menu, you can choose courses in self-realization, meditation, yoga, centering, gestalt therapy, massage, holistic healing, Reichian work, etc, or, you can just come between 1-5pm to relax in the natural baths for $5. Except for these bathing hours, entry is by appointment and pre-arrangement only. The gate guards can be strict and unspiritually obnoxious. It is situated a few miles south of Julia

Pfeiffer Burns State Park. Look for the wooden sign on the west side of the road, and park in the lot at the top, tel. 667-2335.

The writer Henry Miller lived in these hills for 17 years, and wrote lovingly both of the landscape and his neighbors. One of his closest friends was Emile White, a bohemian wanderer from Europe, who Miller encouraged to paint. After Miller's death, White turned his home into the **Henry Miller Memorial Library**, crammed with White's paintings and Miller memorabalia, as well as copies of all sorts of obscure and private publications of Miller's. Across the road from Nepenthe. Open every day, flexible hours, tel. 667-2574. Sales of books and posters help keep the non-profit foundation going.

## Accommodations and food

Lodging in the Big Sur area is generally outrageously overpriced, but this is something one must not allow to deter one from enjoying a vacation in a special place.

*Fernwood*: Lodge, camground and motel units. Restaurant. More reasonable than others, tel. 667-2422.

*Big Sur Lodge*: In Pfeiffer Big Sur State Park. Swimming pool, sauna. Guests have park privileges. Fireplace, kitchen, additional. Starting from $60 for a double, tel. 667-2171.

*The Ventana Inn and Restaurant*: Just south of Pfeiffer Big Sur State Park. The epitome of Big Sur luxury and Big Sur inflation. The cottages are quaint, the views stupendous. The Ventana is raved about for everything, from its latticework to its chocolate torte. Rooms start at $125 for a double. Lunch entrees start at $6, dinner from about $16. Reservations for dinner only. Private campground, tel. 667-2331.

*Gorda*: Towards the southern end of the Big Sur region. The restaurant above the gas station serves dinners that are good, filling, and extremely reasonable, especially for the area. Seafood specials, vegetable quiche, and fine ocean views. $5 and up.

*The Nepenthe*: A well-known local spot with a spectacular view, supposedly where the artists hang out. Entrees from $7 and up. There's dancing around the fire pit in the summer. Open year round, until midnight in summer, tel. 667-2345.

## Important addresses and phone numbers

Area Code: tel. 408 (north) 805 (south).
Emergency: tel. 911.
Big Sur Emergency Road Service: tel. 667-2518.
Gas Stations: River Inn; Ripplewood; Fernwood; Loma Vista; Lucia Lodge; Pacific Valley; Gorda; Ragged Point. Opening hours vary, so it's advisable to keep your tank full.

# *I*NDEX

# *I*NDEX

# *I*NDEX

# NOTES

# NOTES

# NOTES

# *N*OTES

# NOTES

# NOTES

# NOTES

# QUESTIONNAIRE

In our efforts to keep up with the pace and pulse of California, we kindly ask your cooperation in sharing with us any information which you may have as well as your comments. We would greatly appreciate your completing and returning the following questionnaire. Feel free to add additional pages. A complimentary copy of the next edition will be sent to you should any of your suggestions be included.

Our many thanks!

To: Inbal Travel Information (1983) Ltd.
2 Chen Blvd.
Tel Aviv 64071
Israel

Name: _____

Address: _____

_____

Occupation: _____

Date of visit: _____

_____

Purpose of trip (vacation, business, etc.): _____

_____

_____

Comments/Information: _____

_____

_____

_____

_____

_____

_____

_____

_____

_____

_____

_____

_____

_____

**INBAL Travel Information Ltd.**
P.O.B. 39090 Tel Aviv
ISRAEL 61390